MW00615753

Expectations Investing

EXPECTATIONS INVESTING

Reading
Stock Prices
for Better
Returns

MICHAEL J. MAUBOUSSIN
and ALFRED RAPPAPORT

REVISED and UPDATED

Columbia University Press
Publishers Since 1893
New York   Chichester, West Sussex
cup.columbia.edu

Library of Congress Cataloging-in-Publication Data
Names: Mauboussin, Michael J., 1964– author. | Rappaport, Alfred, author.
Title: Expectations investing : reading stock prices for better returns /
Michael J. Mauboussin and Alfred Rappaport.
Description: Revised and Updated Edition. | New York City : Columbia University Press,
2021. | Revised edition of the authors' Expectations investing, c2001.
Identifiers: LCCN 2021015960 (print) | LCCN 2021015961 (ebook) |
ISBN 9780231203043 (hardback) | ISBN 9780231554848 (ebook)
Subjects: LCSH: Investment analysis. | Portfolio management. |
Stocks—Prices.
Classification: LCC HG4529 .R37 2021 (print) | LCC HG4529 (ebook) |
DDC 332.63/2042—dc23
LC record available at https://lccn.loc.gov/2021015960
LC ebook record available at https://lccn.loc.gov/2021015961

Columbia University Press books are printed on permanent
and durable acid-free paper.
Printed in the United States of America

Cover design: Noah Arlow

To Michelle
To Sharon

Contents

Contents

Foreword

ASWATH DAMODARAN

Some ideas are so powerful, and yet so obvious, that when you hear them or read about them for the first time, your inclination is to whack your head and ask yourself why you did not think of them first. That was my reaction when I first read *Expectations Investing*, almost twenty years ago. I was familiar with the authors, having read Al's writings on shareholder value, bridging accounting and value, as well as Michael's research reports that blended psychology, statistics, and common sense to deliver new insights.

As someone who has worked in the valuation trenches for a long time, the book reframed the question of what a company is worth, from estimating value, given fundamentals, to backing out the fundamentals that are embedded in the market price. While there may be little difference mathematically between the two approaches, that reframing accomplishes two missions. The first is that it cements the link between fundamentals and value by linking what the market is paying for a company to what has to happen, in terms of operating success, for that price to be justified, and makes it easier to act on those assessments. The second is that it forces valuation down to the basics, since as Al and Michael show with their parsimonious models, there are only a few levers that drive value.

As I read the new edition of the book, it is clear that Al and Michael are writing a book for the times that we are in, with much more attention paid to disruption, and the value it creates and destroys, and user/subscriber platforms, which can be exploited for gain and thus provide optionality. The section that goes beyond discounted cash flow valuation to look at real options is a must-read for investors and analysts, since it provides not only a tool that can be used to augment intrinsic value but also practical ways of using it. While the Domino's Pizza example is an excellent illustration of the power of expectations investing in traditional value frameworks, the Shopify case study in the real options chapter can be a game changer if you are wondering how you should be valuing technology companies.

I noticed that the foreword to the first edition of this book was written by Peter Bernstein, a man who represented the very best of investment thinking and writing for many decades. I am no Peter Bernstein, but I believe that if he were still alive, he would be writing an even more enthusiastic foreword than he wrote then.

Preface

Stock prices are a treasure of information about the market's expectations of a company's future performance. Investors who properly read market expectations and anticipate revisions increase their odds of achieving superior investment results. Many investors think that they are incorporating expectations when they make decisions, but few actually do so rigorously and explicitly.

The fundamentals of expectations investing are the same as when we published the first version of this book twenty years ago. But plenty in the world is different, making the expectations investing process more useful than ever. Here are some of the most significant changes:

- *A shift from active to passive investing.* Investors have poured trillions into traditional index funds and exchange-traded funds (ETFs) and have withdrawn more than a trillion dollars from actively managed funds since the turn of the century. Index funds and ETFs that track indexes in the United States now have more capital than do funds that pick stocks. Remaining active managers need to embrace the best tools available. We believe that expectations investing provides a path to excess returns.

- *The rise of intangible investments.* In the early 1990s, intangible investments exceeded tangible investments for the first time in the United States. That trend has continued, and companies today invest substantially more in intangible assets than they do in tangible ones. This is important because intangible investments generally appear on the income statement as an expense, while tangible investments are recorded as assets on the balance sheet. Investors have to sort the expenses necessary to support the business from those that are investments in future growth. An understanding of how much a company is investing and whether those investments are likely to create value is essential to anticipating revisions in expectations. Further, scholars have shown that the rise of intangibles has made earnings per share an even less useful measure of corporate performance than it was in the past.

- *A shift from public to private equity.* There are about one-third fewer public companies listed in the United States today than there were in 2001. Over the same time, the venture capital and buyout industries have flourished. Expectations investing provides a framework that investors in both public and private markets can use to improve their chances of finding attractive investment opportunities.

- *Changes in accounting rules.* In the 1990s, stock-based compensation (SBC) consisted primarily of employee stock options that were not expensed on the income statement. Today, SBC is primarily in the form of restricted stock units that are expensed. Both the form of remuneration and how it is accounted for have changed. Further, accounting rules for mergers and acquisitions were revised in 2001, ending the pooling-of-interests method and eliminating goodwill amortization. Expectations investing follows the cash, not earnings, which allows for comparability across companies and over time.

Most investors recognize that the stock valuations that justify their buy and sell decisions are based on expectations for a company's future financial performance. Likewise, corporate executives commonly have projections for sales, operating profit, and the capital needs of their firm for the next three to five years. Investors and corporate executives who adopt expectations investing will have a systematic and robust way to compare their expectations to those of the market.

This book brings the power of expectations investing to portfolio managers, security analysts, investment advisors, individual investors, and business students. Expectations investing has also generated substantial interest in the corporate community. Just as investors can use expectations investing to guide their investment decisions, corporate executives can employ the approach to select an appropriate action to take advantage of mismatches in expectations.

Chapter 1 makes the case for expectations investing and explains why traditional analysis, with its focus on short-term earnings and price-earnings ratios, chases the wrong expectations. In "Gathering the Tools," part I of the book (chapters 2 through 4), we introduce the tools you need to implement expectations investing. Chapter 2 shows that stock market expectations are based on a company's long-term cash flows and demonstrates how to use this model to estimate shareholder value. Chapter 3 introduces the expectations infrastructure, a powerful tool to help investors identify the underlying sources of expectations revisions. Chapter 4 provides competitive strategy frameworks that you can apply to improve your odds of correctly anticipating expectations shifts.

Chapters 5 through 9 (part II, "Implementing the Process") show you how to apply the ideas. Chapters 5, 6, and 7 describe the three steps of the expectations investing process that are the core of the book. Chapter 5 outlines the first step, estimating the market expectations that justify a company's stock price. This step allows investors to harness the power of the discounted cash flow model without bearing the burden of making long-term forecasts. Chapter 6 integrates the tools from the prior chapters to identify potential revisions from current expectations. These revisions are the basis for investment opportunities. Chapter 7, the final step of the process, establishes standards for decisions to buy, sell, and hold a stock. The three steps of the expectations investing process are all you need to analyze the stocks of most companies.

Certain companies, including start-ups and established companies undergoing dramatic change, require additional analysis because the cash flows from existing businesses alone do not justify the stock price. Chapter 8 introduces the real options approach to estimating the potential value of uncertain future opportunities for these companies. Chapter 9 classifies companies into physical, service, or knowledge business categories. While each category has distinct characteristics, we show that expectations investing applies to all companies across the economic landscape.

Finally, in chapters 10 through 12 (part III, "Reading Corporate Signals and Sources of Opportunities"), we examine mergers and acquisitions (M&A), share buybacks, and corporate actions or events that often provide important signals to investors. Chapter 10 shows how to assess an M&A deal by looking beyond earnings and focusing on value and reveals what management's approach to a deal suggests about its prospects. Chapter 11 discusses share buybacks, a topic that is often misunderstood, and features the golden rule of share buybacks. Chapter 12 reviews sources of expectations revision opportunities that have been informed by our experience in applying the expectations investing concepts.

Please visit us at www.expectationsinvesting.com.

Acknowledgments

We are indebted to the team at Counterpoint Global, Morgan Stanley Investment Management, for providing resources and encouragement throughout the project. In particular we want to thank Dennis Lynch and Kristian Heugh. Thomas Kamei provided valuable input to one of our case studies, and Nate Gentile did useful strategic and financial analysis on the Domino's Pizza case study during his internship.

Dan Callahan, a colleague at Counterpoint Global, made enormous contributions to many facets of the book. These include financial analysis, creation of figures and tables, and careful editing. Dan is collaborative, responsive, and diligent. We are grateful for his effort.

Tren Griffin read the full manuscript and encouraged us to sharpen our message.

As a member of the faculty for twenty-eight years at the Kellogg School of Management, Northwestern University, Rappaport would like to acknowledge the benefits of its extraordinarily stimulating environment. Also, his association with the Alcar Group,

Inc., which he cofounded with Carl M. Noble Jr. in 1979, was instrumental in learning how to translate shareholder value from theory to organizational reality.

As a member of the adjunct faculty at Columbia Business School since 1993, Mauboussin thanks the faculty and administration for their support, especially the Heilbrunn Center for Graham & Dodd Investing, as well as the many wonderful students over the years. Many of the revisions in this version of the book were inspired by student interactions.

Authors rarely have the opportunity to update a project after two decades. While we have collaborated on numerous projects in the interim, working on the second version of this book was even more fun than the first one. Writing is a journey that allows for exploring and discovery. We appreciated the trip and the opportunity to learn.

We owe many thanks to the Columbia Business School Publishing team, in particular to our publisher Myles Thompson, who has been unflaggingly enthusiastic about the book from the beginning. Assistant editor Brian Smith steadfastly and efficiently guided us through the publishing process. Ben Kolstad at KnowledgeWorks Global was a wonderful editorial and production partner.

We have admired and learned a great deal from Aswath Damodaran's work over the years and are thrilled that he agreed to contribute the foreword to this edition.

Finally, we enjoyed as always invaluable support from our families. Al thanks his wife, Sharon, his sons Nort and Mitch, and his grandchildren Ilana and Mike. Michael thanks his wife Michelle, his mother-in-law Andrea Maloney Schara, and his wonderful children Andrew, Alex, Madeline, Isabelle, and Patrick.

Expectations Investing

1

The Case for Expectations Investing

STOCK PRICES ARE THE clearest and most reliable signal of the market's expectations about a company's future financial performance. The key to successful investing is to estimate the level of expected performance embedded in the current stock price and then assess the likelihood of a revision in expectations. Most investors agree with these ideas, but very few execute the process properly.

Flip on CNBC or read any popular business magazine and you'll get a familiar story. The growth money manager will explain that she looks for well-managed companies with rapid earnings growth that trade at reasonable price-earnings multiples. The value manager will extol the virtues of buying quality companies at low price-earnings multiples. It happens every day.

But think for a moment about what these investors are really saying. When the growth manager buys a stock, she's betting that the stock market isn't fully reflecting the company's growth prospects. The value manager bets that the market is underestimating the company's intrinsic worth. In both cases, they believe that the market's current expectations are incorrect and are likely to be revised upward.

Although investors do talk about expectations, they're usually talking about the wrong expectations. The mistakes fall into two camps. Investors either don't appreciate the structure of market expectations or they do a poor job of benchmarking expectations.

A focus on short-term earnings is an example of a faulty structure. Short-term earnings are not very helpful for gauging expectations because they are a poor proxy for how the market values stocks. Yet even the investors who embrace an appropriate economic model often miss the mark because they fail to benchmark their expectations against those of the market. It is hard to know where expectations are likely to go tomorrow without knowing where they are today.

The central theme of this book is that the ability to properly read market expectations and anticipate revisions of these expectations is the springboard for earning superior long-term returns. Stock prices express the collective expectations of investors, and changes in those expectations determine investment success.

Seen in this light, stock prices are gifts of information waiting for you to unwrap and use. If you've got a fix on current expectations, you can evaluate where they are likely to go. Like the great hockey player Wayne Gretzky, you can learn to "skate to where the puck is going to be, not to where it has been."[1] That's expectations investing.

In a sharp break from standard practice, expectations investing is a stock-selection process that uses the market's own pricing mechanism, the discounted cash flow model, with an important twist: Rather than forecast cash flows, expectations investing starts by reading the expectations implied by a company's stock price.[2] It also reveals how revisions in expectations affect the stock price. Simply stated, expectations investing uses the right tools to assess the right expectations to make the right investment choice.

Why now? We need to integrate price-implied expectations into our investment decisions because the stakes are now higher than ever. Consider the following:

- Nearly 60 million U.S. households, or almost one in two, own mutual funds. Many more individuals participate in the stock market directly through stock ownership and self-directed retirement accounts or indirectly through pension programs. Around the globe, expectations investing can provide investors with a complete framework for stock selection or, at a minimum, a useful standard by which they can judge the decisions of the portfolio managers they hire.

- Money managers who use outdated analytical tools are at risk of performing poorly and losing assets under management. For example, earnings per share have become even less relevant as intangible investments now exceed tangible investments.

- Expectations investing applies across the economic landscape (physical, service, and knowledge businesses) and across investment styles (growth and value).

- Lured by low or no trading costs, better access to information, and the disappointing record of active managers, some individual investors have shunned mutual funds and are overseeing their own investments. Expectations investing can improve your odds of achieving superior performance if you currently manage your investments or are considering the possibility of doing so.

- More than ever before, assessing major corporate decisions related to merger and acquisition financing, share buybacks, and the issuance of stock-based compensation requires an intelligent examination of their potential impact on a company's stock price. Decisions to issue or repurchase shares might provide the market with a signal to revise its expectations. Expectations investing provides a way to read and assess the reasonableness of those revisions.

Expectations investing is a practical application of corporate finance principles that many companies have used over the decades. The process also incorporates the concepts of value creation and competitive strategy analysis. We integrate these ideas into a powerful toolkit for investors.

Succeeding at active investing is hard. Securities laws around the world seek to provide all investors with material information simultaneously, making it difficult to gain an informational edge. And ongoing innovation, greater global competition, and unforeseen exogenous shocks such as the global pandemic of 2020 have led to a notable increase in uncertainty. Expectations investing translates this heightened uncertainty into opportunity.

Active Management: Challenge and Opportunity

Most institutional and individual investors generate returns on their investment portfolios that are lower than those of passive funds that mirror broad market indexes such as the S&P 500. In fact, about two-thirds of active managers who run funds consisting of large-capitalization stocks lag behind the S&P 500 in an average year, and close to 90 percent underperform over ten years.[3]

Investment performance is a zero-sum game before fees because the gains of investors who beat the market are offset by the losses of investors who underperform the market. In such a world, we expect the skilled investors to gain and the unskilled to lose. But the task is becoming even more difficult. For example, the standard deviation of excess returns, which measures the difference between the results of the best and worst managers, has narrowed consistently since the 1970s. Even as the absolute skill of investors has risen, the relative skill between investors has declined.[4]

Why do institutional investors underperform passive benchmarks? Does active management really pay? If so, then what approach offers the best chance of delivering superior returns?

Before we address these questions, here's the bottom line: The disappointing performance of professionally managed funds is not an indictment of active management per se, but rather reflects the suboptimal strategies that many active professionals use.[5] We believe that expectations investing offers a powerful process for achieving superior returns.

Let's be clear. Active investing is not easy. You should choose low-cost index and exchange-traded funds if you want to avoid underperforming the market and broad market returns satisfy you. Even the most astute and diligent investors struggle to beat the market consistently, and expectations investing offers no shortcut to riches. But its approach will help all active investors reach their potential.

Now let's look at the four primary reasons that institutional investors underperform passive benchmarks: tools, costs, incentives, and style limitations. We'll see how expectations investing alleviates each of these constraints.

Tools

Standard practice: Most investors use accounting-based tools such as short-term earnings and price-earnings multiples. These measures are inherently flawed and are becoming even less useful as companies increasingly depend on intangible rather than tangible assets to create value. We expand on the shortcomings of earnings as poor proxies for market expectations in the last section of this chapter.

Expectations investing draws from finance theory to pinpoint the market's expectations. It then taps appropriate competitive strategy frameworks to help investors anticipate revisions in expectations.

Costs

Standard practice: The late John Bogle, founder of The Vanguard Group, correlates costs to mutual fund performance, averring that "the surest route to top-quartile returns is bottom-quartile expenses."[6] The asset-weighted expense ratio for actively managed U.S. equity mutual funds averages about 0.68 percent of asset value. In contrast, the equivalent expense ratio for passive funds is 0.09 percent of asset value.[7]

Expectations investing establishes demanding standards for buying and selling stocks, resulting in lower stock portfolio turnover, reduced transaction costs, and decreased taxes.

Incentives

Standard practice: Fund shareholders generally compare their returns quarterly to a benchmark such as the S&P 500. Fund managers commonly fear that they will lose substantial assets, and potentially their jobs, if they fail to achieve acceptable short-term performance. The inability to sustain pain in the short term can affect the opportunity to achieve superior gains in the long term. Many managers naturally obsess over short-term relative returns.

The result has been a shift from identifying mispriced stocks to minimizing the variance from the benchmark. Indeed, active share, a measure of how different portfolios are from their benchmarks, has declined steadily in recent decades. This blunts the odds of outperforming benchmark indexes and index funds.

Expectations investing improves the probability of beating the benchmark over longer periods, provided that the fund manager can buck the system and embrace more effective analytical tools.

Style Limitations

Standard practice: Most professional money managers classify their investing style as either growth or value. Growth managers focus on companies that rapidly increase sales and profits and generally trade at high price-earnings multiples. Value managers seek stocks that trade at substantial discounts to their expected value and often have low price-earnings multiples. Significantly, industry consultants discourage money managers from drifting from their stated style, limiting the universe of acceptable stocks.

Expectations investing doesn't distinguish between growth and value. Portfolio managers simply pursue maximum long-term returns within a specified investment policy. As Warren Buffett convincingly argues, "Market commentators and investment managers who glibly refer to 'growth' and 'value' styles as contrasting approaches to investment are displaying their ignorance, not their sophistication. Growth is simply a component—usually a plus, sometimes a minus—in the value equation."[8]

Expectations investing not only helps identify undervalued stocks to buy or hold, but it also identifies overvalued stocks to avoid or sell in the investor's target universe.

Does expectations investing offer insightful, dedicated investors a reasonable probability of achieving superior returns? We think so.

In 1976, Jack Treynor, who was a prominent leader in the investment industry, distinguished between ideas "whose implications are straightforward and obvious" and "those that require reflection, judgment, special expertise, etc., for their evaluation." The latter idea, he argued, is "the only meaningful definition for 'long-term investing.' "[9]

When companies announce earnings surprises, mergers and acquisitions, a new drug, or a government antitrust action, the long-term valuation implications are rarely obvious. Investors quickly assess the favorable or unfavorable effects on the current price, and they trade accordingly. Not surprisingly, trading volume typically increases following these announcements. Volatile stock prices and increased trading volume affirm that investors quickly respond to such information. But what distinguishes the winners from the losers is not how quickly they respond but how well they interpret the information. Investors interpret the same information differently, and some interpretations are better than others.

In other words, stock prices quickly reflect revised, but perhaps miscalculated, expectations. To succeed, investors must first skillfully read expectations and then use the best available tools to decide whether and how today's expectations will change. Welcome to expectations investing.

The Expectations Investing Process

In the following chapters, we'll walk you carefully through the three-step process of expectations investing.

Step 1: Estimate Price-Implied Expectations

We first read the expectations embedded in a stock with a long-term discounted cash flow model. We thus reverse the common practice, which begins with earnings or cash flow forecasts to estimate value. The benefits of this reverse engineering include the following:

- The long-term discounted cash flow model is the right tool to read expectations because it mirrors the way the market prices stocks.
- Expectations investing solves a dilemma that investors face in a world of heightened uncertainty by allowing them to harness the power of the discounted cash flow model without forecasting long-term cash flows.

- Investors can be agnostic about the investment opportunity because the goal is to simply understand what financial expectations are priced in by the market.

Step 2: Identify Expectations Opportunities

Once we estimate current expectations, we apply the appropriate strategic and financial tools to determine where and when revisions in expectations are likely to occur. Here are the advantages
of this approach:

- Expectations investing is a methodology that reveals whether
  the stock price is most sensitive to revisions in the company's sales, operating costs, or investment needs. This allows
  investors to focus on the potential revisions that matter
  most.
- Expectations investing applies the best available competitive strategy frameworks in the investor's search for potential expectations revisions.
- Expectations investing provides the tools to evaluate all
  public or private companies, including those that rely on
  tangible or intangible assets, value or growth, developed
  or emerging markets, and start-ups or established businesses. Expectations investing applies universally.

Step 3: Buy, Sell, or Hold?

Finally, the process defines clear standards for buy and sell decisions. Central features include the following:

- Prospective buys must offer a clear-cut "margin of safety,"
  a sufficient discount to expected value so as to compensate
  for the potential of analytical mistakes or bad luck. Likewise, a sell candidate must trade at a sufficient premium to
  its expected value.

- Key insights from behavioral finance help investors avoid decision-making pitfalls.
- The use of demanding buy-and-sell hurdles reduces transaction costs and income taxes.

The Twilight of Traditional Analysis

In 1938, John Burr Williams published a book called *The Theory of Investment Value*, a seminal articulation of the usefulness of the discounted cash flow model to establish value. Williams convincingly addressed investor concerns that the long-term discounted cash flow model is too intricate, uncertain, and impractical.[10] Notwithstanding the extraordinary advances in financial theory since then, many investors still eschew the model and the full cadre of available financial and strategic tools to implement it.

The full demonstration of expectations investing in the following chapters will reveal its superiority to widely used investment tools. But three pervasive misconceptions in the investment community deserve special mention:

1. The market takes a short-term view.
2. Earnings per share (EPS) dictate value.
3. Price-earnings multiples determine value.

These fallacies lead investors to chase the wrong expectations and can result in poor performance. Let's examine each.

Belief: The Market Takes a Short-Term View
Reality: The Market Takes a Long-Term View

Most investors and corporate managers believe that short-term reported earnings rather than long-term cash flows are the basis for stock prices. Why? There are three plausible explanations.

The first is a misinterpretation of the stock market's response to earnings announcements. The stock price changes when quarterly earnings announcements provide investors with new information about a company's long-term cash flow prospects. But the market is not reacting mechanically to reported earnings. Rather, it uses unexpected earnings results, and increasingly management's guidance about future earnings, as a signal to revise expectations for a company's future cash flows when appropriate. If the market interprets disappointing earnings or guidance as a sign of a downturn over the long term, it sends the stock price lower.[11]

Second, the stocks of businesses with excellent long-term prospects do not always deliver superior shareholder returns. Shareholders of a company with a stock price that fully anticipates its performance should expect to earn a market-required rate of return. The way astute investors can earn superior returns is by anticipating shifts in a company's competitive position and the resulting changes in cash flows that the current stock price does not reflect.

Finally, commentators frequently point to relatively short investor holding periods to support their belief that the market is oriented to the short term. For example, high-frequency trading and quantitative funds are more prominent today than in prior generations even as asset-weighted mutual fund turnover has drifted lower since the dot-com peak in 2000.[12] How can investors who hold a stock for months, or even days, care about a company's long-term outlook?

The simple answer to this apparent conundrum is that investor holding periods are different from the market's investment time horizon. To understand the horizon, you must look at stock prices, not investor holding periods. Studies confirm that you need to extend expected cash flows over many years to justify stock prices. Investors make short-term bets on long-term outcomes.

How do we know that the market takes the long view? The most direct evidence comes from stock prices themselves. We can estimate the expected level and duration of cash flows that today's price implies. As it turns out, most companies need over ten years of value-creating cash flows to justify their stock price.

Indirect evidence comes from the percentage of today's stock price that we can attribute to dividends expected over the next five years. Only about 10 to 15 percent of the price of stocks in the Dow Jones Industrial Average comes from expected dividends for the next five years.[13]

Belief: Earnings per Share (EPS) Dictate Value
Reality: Earnings Tell Us Little About Value

The investment community and corporate managers undeniably fixate on EPS. For example, academics who surveyed chief financial officers about financial reporting summarized the responses by stating, "Earnings are king."[14] The *Wall Street Journal* and other media outlets spend a lot of time talking about sales growth, quarterly earnings per share, and price-earnings multiples. This broad dissemination and frequent market reactions to earnings announcements might lead some to believe that reported earnings strongly influence, if not totally determine, stock prices.

The profound differences between earnings and long-term cash flows, however, not only underscore why earnings are such a poor proxy for expectations, but also show why upward earnings revisions do not necessarily increase stock prices. The shortcomings of earnings include the following:

- Earnings exclude a charge for the cost of capital.
- Earnings exclude the incremental investments in working capital and fixed capital needed to support a company's growth.
- Companies can compute earnings using alternative, equally acceptable accounting methods.

Discounted cash flow models and stock prices account for the time value of money: A dollar today is worth more than a dollar a year from now because we can invest today's dollar to earn a return over the next year. When a company invests, it must compare its return to those of alternative, equally risky investment opportunities. This opportunity cost, or cost of capital, is the discount rate for a discounted cash flow model. Earnings calculations, in contrast, ignore this opportunity cost and the time value of money.

In a discounted cash flow model, value increases only when the company earns a rate of return on new investments that exceeds the cost of capital. The important insight is that a company can grow earnings without investing at or above the cost of capital. (The appendix at the end of this chapter provides a detailed example.) Consequently, higher earnings do not always translate into higher value.

Consider the second difference, the required investments in working capital and fixed capital. Earnings do not recognize the cash outflows for investments in future growth, such as increases in accounts receivable, inventory, and fixed assets. Discounted cash flow models, in contrast, incorporate all cash inflows and outflows. For example, Shake Shack, a fast-casual restaurant chain, reported net income of $24.1 million in 2019, whereas its cash flow was negative $16.7 million (table 1.1). The first figure tells you very little about the second one, in either the short or the long term.

Finally, companies can use a wide range of permissible methods to determine earnings. How accountants record a business event does not alter the event or its impact on shareholder value.

Enlightened accountants readily acknowledge that neither they nor their conventions have a comparative advantage in valuing a business. The role of corporate financial reporting is to provide useful information for estimating value.

Revenue recognition and matching expenses with revenue are the two fundamental steps that determine earnings. A company recognizes revenue when it delivers products or services and can

Table 1.1
Reconciliation of earnings and cash flow for Shake Shack Inc. (2019, in thousands)

	Earnings	Adjustment	Cash flow
Sales	$594,519		
+ Change in accounts receivable		10,726	$605,245
Cost of revenue	(446,607)		
– Increase in other assets		(8,583)	
+ Increase in other liabilities		(19,595)	(474,785)
+ Depreciation and amortization expense		40,704	
– Noncash lease cost		40,068	
– Capital expenditures		(106,507)	(25,735)
+ Stock-based compensation		7,505	
General and administrative	(65,649)		
Depreciation	(40,392)		
Pre-opening costs	(14,834)		
Other	(1,352)	968	(113,754)
Other income, net	2,263		
Interest expense	(434)		1,829
Income tax expense	(3,386)		
– Deferred taxes		(6,064)	
Stock option tax benefits			
Reported net income	$24,128		
Cash flow			($16,650)

Source: Shake Shack Inc. 2019 Form 10-K.

reasonably establish the amount that it will collect from customers. It then expenses the costs needed to generate that revenue during the period in which it recognizes the revenue. In other words, it matches expenses with revenues. This matching principle is easy to grasp in concept but can be hopelessly arbitrary in implementation.

Accounting standards give companies latitude in revenue recognition, depreciation methods, and inventory accounting, to name a few.

Belief: Price-Earnings Multiples Determine Value
Reality: Price-Earnings Multiples Are a Function of Value

The investment community's favorite valuation metric is the price-earnings (P/E) multiple.[15] A measure of what investors will pay for a stock, the multiple equals the stock price (P) divided by a company's earnings per share (E). Investors incorporate it in a deceptively simple valuation formula:

$$\text{Shareholder value per share} = \text{Earnings per share} \times \text{P/E}$$

Since an estimate of earnings per share (EPS) is available, investors must decide only on the appropriate multiple to determine a stock's value and then compare the result to the stock's current price and assess whether it is undervalued, overvalued, or fairly valued. The calculation is easy, but the results are disappointing.

Look closely at the formula. Since we know last year's EPS or next year's consensus EPS estimate, we need only estimate the appropriate P/E. But since we have the denominator (earnings per share, or E), the only unknown is the appropriate share price, or P. We are therefore left with a useless tautology: To estimate value, we require an estimate of value.

This flawed logic underscores the fundamental point: The price-earnings multiple does not determine value but rather derives from value. Price-earnings analysis is not an analytical shortcut. It is an economic cul-de-sac.

Essential Ideas

- Investors who can read the market's expectations and anticipate changes in those expectations will more likely generate superior investment returns.

- The expectations investing approach harnesses the powerful discounted cash flow model but starts with price and then solves for cash flow expectations.
- Investors who play the earnings expectations game are likely to lose because short-term earnings do not reflect how the market prices stocks.

Appendix: Earnings Growth and Value Creation

Let's look at why earnings growth and shareholder value growth are not synonymous. Consider Earnings Growth, Incorporated (EGI). To simplify calculations, assume that EGI has no debt and requires no incremental investment. Earnings and cash flow are therefore identical. These simplifying assumptions do not affect the conclusions of the analysis. EGI's most recent year's income statement is as follows:

	($ in millions)
Sales	$100
Operating expenses	85
Operating profit (15%)	15
Taxes (20%)	3
Earnings	$12

Suppose the company maintains its present sales level and margins for the foreseeable future. With an 8 percent cost of equity capital, EGI's shareholder value is $12 million divided by 8 percent, or $150 million.

Now let's say that EGI has the opportunity to invest $15 million of its internally generated cash today, which will allow it to expand sales by 10 percent while maintaining pretax margins at

15 percent. Here is EGI's projected income statement for next year and subsequent years:

	($ in millions)
Sales	$110.0
Operating expenses	93.5
Operating profit (15%)	16.5
Taxes (20%)	3.3
Earnings	$13.2

EGI's shareholder value is now $165 million ($13.2 million divided by 8 percent) minus the $15 million investment, or $150 million ($165 – $15 = $150). Note that despite 10 percent earnings growth, shareholder value remains the same because the $15 million investment increases annual after-tax cash flow by $1.2 million, which, when discounted at 8 percent, is worth exactly $15 million. Shareholder value doesn't change when the present value of incremental cash inflow is identical to the present value of the investment.

When new investments yield a return below the cost of capital, shareholder value decreases even as earnings increase. For example, assume that EGI's sales growth next year will be 20 percent with a $30 million investment. However, the pretax margin on incremental sales will be 10 percent, rather than the 15 percent rate projected earlier. Here is the revised income statement for next year and subsequent years:

	($ in millions)
Sales	$120.0
Operating expenses	103.0
Operating profit	17.0
Taxes (20%)	3.4
Earnings	$13.6

While earnings grow from $12 million to $13.6 million, or 13.3 percent, shareholder value is $170 million ($13.6 million divided by 8 percent) minus the $30 million investment, or $140 million. Even though earnings grow, there is a $10 million decrease in value ($140 − $150 = −$10).

Stock prices relate tenuously to earnings growth. Instead, changes in expectations about future cash flows drive changes in shareholder value and stock price. So reported earnings growth, even when accompanied by increases in shareholder value, can trigger reduced investor expectations and a fall in the stock price.

PART I

Gathering the Tools

2

How the Market Values Stocks

TRADITIONAL DISCOUNTED cash flow analysis requires you to forecast cash flows to estimate a stock's value. Expectations investing reverses the process. It starts with the stock price, a rich and underutilized source of information, and determines the cash flow expectations that justify that price. Those expectations, in turn, serve as the benchmark for decisions to buy, sell, or hold a stock.

Before we go too far down the expectations investing path, we need to be certain that we are tracking the right expectations. We must therefore answer an essential question: Do prices in financial markets truly reflect expected future cash flows?

The Right Expectations

We return to first principles to see why the stock market bases its expectations on long-term cash flows. A dollar today is worth more than a dollar in the future because you can invest today's dollar and earn a positive rate of return. This process is called compounding. The reverse of compounding is discounting, which converts a future cash flow into its equivalent present value. An asset's present value is the sum of its expected cash flows discounted by an expected rate of return. That return is what investors anticipate earning on assets with similar risk. The present value is the maximum price an investor should pay for an asset.[1]

The discounted cash flow model sets prices in all well-functioning capital markets, including those for bonds and real estate. For example, bond issuers contractually establish a coupon rate, principal repayment, and maturity. Bond prices are the present value of the contractual cash flows discounted at the current expected rate of return. When the inflationary outlook or a company's credit quality prompts a higher or lower expected rate, the prices of its bonds change accordingly. The market sets prices so that expected returns match the perceived risk.

The discounted cash flow model also dominates pricing in the commercial real estate market. When the Empire State Building went up for sale in the early 1990s, real estate experts pegged its market value at around $450 million. Yet the purchase price was a scant $40 million because of the building's long-term master lease, which had a rate below that of the market. Neither its marquee name nor its prime location set the Empire State Building's price. Its discounted cash flow value did.[2]

Given that the magnitude, timing, and riskiness of cash flows determine the value of bonds and real estate, we can expect these variables to dictate stock prices as well. The problem is that the inputs for stocks are much less certain. Whereas bonds contractually specify cash flows and a date when principal is to be repaid, stocks have uncertain cash flows, an indefinite life, and no provision for repayment. That greater uncertainty makes stocks more difficult to value than bonds.

Does that mean that we shouldn't value stocks with discounted cash flow? Certainly not. After all, the returns that investors receive when they purchase any financial asset depend on the cash flows that they receive while owning the asset plus their proceeds when selling it. John Bogle, whom we met in chapter 1, argues for discounted cash flow valuation: "Sooner or later, the rewards of investing *must* be based on future cash flows. The purpose of any stock market, after all, is simply to provide liquidity for stocks in return for the promise of future cash flows, enabling investors to realize the present value of a future stream of income at any time."[3]

Extensive empirical research demonstrates that the market determines the prices of stocks just as it does any other financial asset. Specifically, the studies show two relationships. First, market prices respond to changes in a company's prospects for cash flow. Second, market prices reflect cash flows well into the future. As noted before, companies often need ten years of value-creating cash flows to justify their stock price. This period can be as long as twenty years for companies with formidable competitive advantages.

Yet most money managers, security analysts, and individual investors avoid the difficulty of forecasting long-term cash flows altogether. They instead focus on near-term earnings, price-earnings ratios, or similar metrics. Such measures can help identify undervalued stocks only when they are reliable proxies for a company's long-term cash flow prospects. But static measures of near-term performance do not capture future performance and ultimately let investors down, especially in a global economy marked by spirited competition and disruptive technologies. An investor cannot convincingly conclude that a stock is undervalued or overvalued without assessing a company's future cash flows.

Shareholder Value Road Map

We need to define cash flow and show how it leads to a calculation of shareholder value. Figure 2.1 depicts the shareholder value

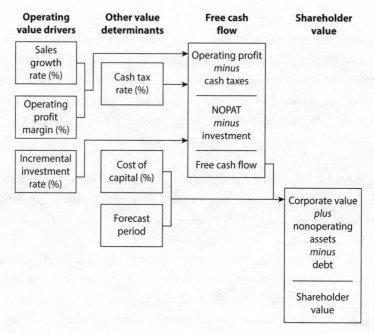

FIGURE 2.1 The shareholder value road map.

road map and serves as a guide for estimating shareholder value. It reveals the following relationships:

- Sales growth and operating profit margin determine operating profit.
- Operating profit minus cash taxes yields net operating profit after taxes (NOPAT).
- NOPAT minus investments in working and fixed capital equals free cash flow. Think of free cash flow as the pool of cash available to pay the claims of debtholders and shareholders.
- Free cash flows discounted at the cost of capital determine corporate value.

- Corporate value plus nonoperating assets minus the market value of debt and other relevant liabilities equals shareholder value.

These relationships describe the standard discounted cash flow process that estimates cash flows in order to determine shareholder value. Expectations investing reverses the process by starting with price, which may differ from value, and determines the expectations for cash flows that the price implies.

Free Cash Flow

Conveniently, we can use familiar financial statement variables to estimate the market's expectations for future free cash flows. Take another look at figure 2.1. Three operating value drivers—sales growth, operating profit margin, and incremental investment rate—and one value determinant, cash tax rate, determine free cash flow. We consider sales growth, operating profit margin, and incremental investment rate to be operating value drivers because they are significantly influenced by management decisions. Value determinants are dictated by external forces such as the government and financial markets.

Here's how to calculate free cash flow for the first year of a forecast period. Assume that last year's sales were $100 million and that expectations for next year are as follows:

Sales growth rate	10%
Operating profit margin	15%
Cash tax rate	25%
Incremental fixed-capital investment	$1.50 million
Incremental working-capital investment	$1.00 million

We compute free cash flow as follows:

Sales	$110.00 million
Operating profit = Sales × 15%	16.50
Less: Cash taxes = Operating profit ×	(4.13)
Cash tax rate = 16.50 × 25%	
NOPAT	12.38
Incremental fixed-capital investment	(1.50)
Incremental working-capital investment	(1.00)
Less: Total investment	(2.50)
Free cash flow	$9.88 million

The sales number is the same as the top line of the income statement. The sales growth rate is simply the year-to-year percentage change. Operating profit margin is the ratio of pre-interest, pre-tax operating profit to sales. Because we want to calculate cash flow, we exclude the amortization of acquired intangible assets, which is a noncash expense. We also exclude the embedded interest in lease expense, as that is appropriately considered a financing cost.[4] Depreciation expense remains as part of the operating profit margin calculation even though it is a noncash item. But we don't forget about it: We deduct it from capital expenditures so that free cash flow is truly a cash figure.

On to taxes. The tax expense in the income statement, book taxes, is often greater than the actual payments, or cash taxes, during a given period. This is because companies can recognize some revenue and expense items at different times for book versus tax purposes.

For example, a company may use straight-line depreciation for book purposes and an accelerated depreciation method for tax purposes. Since accelerated depreciation is greater than straight-line depreciation, it increases a company's expenses and reduces its cash tax bill. Stock-based compensation can also create timing differences between cash and reported taxes. As a result, cash tax rates are commonly lower than book tax rates.[5]

The cash tax rate represents taxes payable on operating profit, not on pretax income. Therefore, to calculate the taxes that a company would pay if it were entirely equity financed, we must remove the tax effects of interest expense and nonoperating income or expenses. Removing the tax benefit of interest expense deductions, interest expense multiplied by the tax rate, increases the cash tax bill, and removing the taxes on nonoperating income reduces the taxes on operating profit.

We now arrive at net operating profit after taxes (NOPAT). To complete the journey to free cash flow, we must subtract incremental investments. An investment is an outlay today with the expectation that it will generate cash flows in the future that make the investment economically worthwhile. Standard items include fixed-capital investment, changes in operating working capital, and acquisitions.

Let's begin with fixed-capital investment, which captures capital expenditures and depreciation expense. For insights into market expectations, we should use a publicly available service that provides long-term forecasts, such as the *Value Line Investment Survey* and analyst projections, to estimate a company's incremental fixed-capital investment rate. This rate is the fixed-capital investment required per dollar of sales increase. We calculate it as capital expenditures minus depreciation expense divided by the change in sales forecasted for the same period.[6]

We deduct depreciation because it reasonably approximates the required spending to maintain current productive capacity. As a result, we consider only capital investment above and beyond depreciation as an incremental investment. For example, if this rate is 15 percent, then a sales increase from $100 million to $110 million in the first year will produce an incremental fixed-capital investment of $1.50 million (15 percent = $1.50 million/$10 million).

The extent to which historical investment rates are useful for assessing expectations depends on a number of factors. These include the relative stability of a company's product mix, technological changes, and the company's ability to offset increased fixed-capital costs through higher selling prices or more efficient use of fixed assets. The historical investment rate, adjusted for relevant information, is a useful starting point for judging the reasonableness of the forecasted rate.

Changes in operating working capital relative to changes in sales define a company's incremental working-capital investment rate. Operating working capital equals current assets minus non-interest-bearing current liabilities. Current assets are primarily accounts receivable and inventory, and non-interest-bearing current liabilities are mainly accounts payable and accrued liabilities. Current assets should exclude cash beyond what the company needs to run its operations. As a business grows, operating working capital generally grows proportionally.

The rate is the change in working capital expressed as a percentage of the change in sales. For instance, if the incremental working-capital investment rate is 10 percent, then a sales increase of $10 million will lead to an incremental working-capital investment of $1.00 million (10 percent = $1.00 million/$10 million).

Changes in working capital underscore another difference between earnings and cash flow. For example, an increase in accounts receivable from the beginning to the end of a year indicates that a company received less cash during the year than the recorded sales suggest. For accounting purposes, companies recognize sales when they deliver goods or services, but for valuation purposes what matters is when the companies receive cash.

Inventories also generally rise as sales increase. Rising inventory requires cash payments for materials, labor, and overhead. Since cost of goods sold excludes the cash outlays for additional inventory, we must include it as a working-capital investment.

The final component of working capital, accounts payable and accrued liabilities, counterbalances receivables and inventory. Payables and accrued liabilities represent unpaid bills for expenses already deducted on the income statement. Since companies disburse cash after they recognize some of their expenses, increases in payables reduce the current year's cash outlays and investment in working capital.

Indeed, some businesses have non-interest-bearing current liabilities that exceed current assets, which means that working capital can be a source of cash as long as growth continues. Amazon.com is a prominent example of a company that has used working capital to finance its expansion. Because the company receives cash from its customers before it has to pay its suppliers, working capital has been a source of cash rather than an investment outlay. Companies consistently spend substantially more on mergers and acquisitions (M&A) than on fixed and working capital. Chapter 10 is dedicated to M&A in recognition of its significance to capital allocation. We limit the discussion here to fixed and working capital investment because the timing, size, and success of M&A deals are difficult to forecast.

Any discussion of incremental investments requires an acknowledgment that intangible investments have grown more rapidly than tangible investments in recent decades. Because intangible investments are expensed, the investments companies make are increasingly showing up on the income statement rather than on the balance sheet. For example, applying one researcher's assumptions to fiscal 2020 results, Microsoft spent $34.0 billion on research and development and other intangible investments and $15.4 billion on capital expenditures.[7] What is important is that free cash flow is not affected by where accountants record investments.

The free cash flows over the forecast period represent only a fraction of a company's value. After all, its cash flows don't just mysteriously disappear at the end of the forecast period.

Continuing value, the value of free cash flows after the forecast period, often constitutes the majority of a company's total value. Continuing value is also known as terminal, or residual, value.

What is the best way to estimate continuing value? We recommend matching the business you are analyzing with one of four methods: perpetuity, perpetuity-with-inflation, perpetuity-with-partial-inflation, or perpetuity-with-decline. (The appendix at the end of this chapter will help you determine which method to use.) The first three approaches assume that a company generating returns greater than its cost of capital will attract competition that will ultimately drive returns down to the cost of capital by the end of the forecast period. Further, they assume that a company can sustain the NOPAT it earns at the end of the forecast period and that future investments do not create value. The methods do not suggest that a company will not grow. They suggest only that additional growth will not add to shareholder value.

The fourth method, perpetuity-with-decline, anticipates that NOPAT will shrink over time. This is appropriate for companies within industries in decline.

The perpetuity method implies that NOPAT remains constant in nominal terms. The perpetuity-with-inflation method assumes that free cash flow will grow at the rate of inflation in the post-forecast period, which suggests that NOPAT remains level in real terms.[8] The perpetuity-with-partial-inflation implies that the company will be able to maintain some pricing power. No single continuing value method is appropriate in all circumstances, and the method you choose should be consistent with your assumptions about the business's competitive position at the end of the forecast period.[9]

We now know how to take familiar financial statement metrics and translate them into free cash flow. To convert free cash flows to corporate value, we need to estimate an appropriate discount rate, the cost of capital.

FINANCIAL INSTITUTIONS

In this chapter, we recommend that you use the enterprise discounted cash flow method to read market expectations. This approach uses estimates to determine corporate value, adds cash and other non-operating assets, and subtracts debt to calculate shareholder value. It is appropriate for nonfinancial companies.

In contrast, the best way for you to read expectations for financial services companies is with the equity discounted cash flow method. Financial services companies, such as banks, insurance companies, and brokers, represented about 13 percent of the stocks in the S&P 500 at year-end 2020. The equity approach discounts future free cash flows for shareholders at the cost of equity capital. Since financial services companies use the liability side of the balance sheet to create value, the equity approach, though mathematically equivalent to the enterprise method, is more straightforward.

Further, even within financial services, different business models require different approaches. For example, the model you need to read the expectations for a bank is different from what you need for an insurance company.

Despite these distinctions, the expectations investing techniques we develop throughout this book apply to all companies. However, you may need to adapt the appropriate model slightly to best understand the expectations built into the stocks of financial services companies.

Cost of Capital

The weighted average cost of capital, which includes both debt and equity, is the appropriate rate for discounting free cash flows. For example, suppose you estimate that a company's after-tax cost of debt is 4.0 percent and that its cost of equity is 9.0 percent. It plans to raise capital in the proportion of 20 percent debt and 80 percent equity. You calculate the cost of capital as follows:

	Weight (%)	Cost (%)	Weighted cost (%)
Debt (after-tax)	20	4.0	0.80
Equity	80	9.0	<u>7.20</u>
Cost of capital			8.00

The cost of capital incorporates the expected returns of both debtholders and shareholders since both groups have claims on free cash flow. This is appropriate because free cash flow is calculated before interest expense. The weighted average cost of capital considers each group's claims in proportion to the expected contribution to the financing of the company.

You should use market value, not book value, to calculate weights for target capital structure because debtholders and shareholders expect to earn competitive rates of return on the market value of their stakes.[10] Book values reflect historical costs that generally do not correspond to market values and therefore are not relevant to today's investment decisions.

How do you estimate the costs of debt and equity? Measuring the cost of debt is straightforward because debt is a contractual obligation to pay a specific rate. The cost of debt is the rate that a company would have to pay today on its long-term debt. Since interest expense on debt is tax deductible, you can use this formula to find the after-tax cost of debt-financed instruments for a company:[11]

Yield-to-maturity on long-term debt × (1 – Tax rate)

Estimating the cost of equity is more difficult because companies do not agree to pay their common shareholders an explicit rate of return. Nonetheless, investors require an implicit rate of return to purchase or to hold a company's shares.

Rational investors expect to earn a rate of return proportionate with the risk they assume. Risk is, after all, the price that investors pay for opportunity. What rate of return is necessary to induce investors to buy a company's shares? One logical starting place is the sum of the risk-free rate and an additional return for investing in more risky stocks, or an equity risk premium:[12]

Equation 2.1:

Cost of equity = Risk-free rate + Equity risk premium

Even government securities are not entirely risk-free. While essentially free of default risk, they are subject to increases in interest rates and the resulting losses in value. In the absence of a truly riskless security, we can use the rate of return on U.S. ten-year Treasury notes, or comparable sovereign debt, to estimate the risk-free rate.

The equity risk premium is the second component of the cost of equity. The equity risk premium for an individual stock is the product of the market risk premium for equity and an individual stock's systematic risk as measured by its beta coefficient:[13]

Equation 2.2:

Equity risk premium = Beta × Market risk premium

The beta coefficient assesses how sensitive a stock's return is to overall market movements. The beta on a market portfolio is 1.0. Stocks with betas greater than 1.0 are more volatile than the market and thus have equity risk premiums greater than the market risk premium. For example, if a stock moves up or down 1.25 percent when the market moves up or down 1 percent, then it has a beta of 1.25. Likewise, stocks with positive betas of less than 1.0 move in the same direction as the market, but not as far. You can obtain betas from several sources, including *Bloomberg*, *FactSet*, and *Value Line*.

The final variable, the market risk premium, is the additional return that investors expect for holding a well-diversified portfolio of stocks rather than risk-free government debt securities. To estimate the market risk premium, subtract the risk-free rate from the expected rate of return on a representative market index such as the S&P 500:

Equation 2.3:

Market risk premium = Expected market rate of return –
Risk-free rate

Investors should base the market risk premium on expected rates of return, not on historical rates. Investors who use historical rates ignore the fact that market risk premiums vary over time. Forward-looking approaches, as well as more recent historical data, suggest an equity risk premium in the range of 4 to 6 percent.[14]

Equation 2.4 puts all the pieces together and provides the formula to calculate the cost of equity.

Equation 2.4:

Cost of equity = Risk-free rate + Beta × (Expected market rate of
return – Risk-free rate)

For example, if we assume a 1.5 percent risk-free rate, a beta of 1.25, and a 7.5 percent expected return on the market, the cost of equity would be as follows:

Cost of equity = 1.5% + 1.25(7.5% – 1.5%) = 9.0%

Forecast Period

Turn again to figure 2.1 to understand the importance of the forecast period. Free cash flow discounted at the cost of capital determines today's value of future free cash flows. We need to assess how many years of free cash flow the market impounds in a stock price.

We disagree with valuation texts that advocate arbitrary five- or ten-year periods. The forecast period is the time that the market expects a company to generate returns on incremental investment that exceed its cost of capital. Economic theory and empirical results show that companies that generate excess returns attract competition that eventually drives returns toward the cost of capital.

Analysts typically choose a forecast period that is too short when they perform discounted cash flow valuations. You're missing the point if you believe that a forecast beyond two or three years smacks of sheer speculation. Market prices do reflect long-term cash flow expectations. In fact, historical prices in the stock market suggest a market-implied forecast period of between five and fifteen years.[15]

Of course, market-implied forecast periods differ for various industries. We also find that implied forecast periods for companies within an industry tend to cluster, although these periods can change over time. In chapter 5, we will show precisely how to estimate the market-implied forecast period. The key thing to remember for now is that the stock market takes a long-term view.

From Corporate Value to Shareholder Value

The present value of free cash flows for the forecast period plus the continuing value equals corporate value. Shareholder value equals corporate value plus nonoperating assets minus debt.

You might wonder why our calculation of shareholder value incorporates nonoperating assets such as excess cash, marketable securities, and other investments not essential to daily operations. It does because they have value and because we excluded the cash they will generate from the calculation of free cash flow. Excess cash is the cash above and beyond what a company needs for current operations. Companies sometimes stockpile cash and marketable securities to weather an industry downturn or to prepare for a large acquisition.

Nonoperating assets can represent a significant percentage of a company's stock price. For example, Microsoft, Berkshire Hathaway, Alphabet, and Apple each had more than $100 billion in cash and marketable securities at year-end 2020.[16] Some nonoperating assets have taxable gains, so it's also important to make sure you consider taxes when you place a value on them. Research shows that cash holdings are sensitive to tax policies.[17]

The cash requirements for a company's daily operations vary from industry to industry. In general, more stable and mature businesses require a small amount, about 1 percent of sales, and less stable and young businesses require an amount closer to 5 to 10 percent of sales.

Finally, we subtract the market value of debt to obtain shareholder value. Debt includes not only bonds but also preferred stock and underfunded pension plans.[18] We deduct the value of preferred stock because a company must ordinarily pay preferred dividends in full before it can distribute cash to its common shareholders. We deduct the pension plan liability when the present value of projected pension benefit obligations is greater than plan assets. Because sponsoring companies are ultimately responsible for the underfunding, you should deduct the underfunded balance to determine shareholder value.[19]

Summary Illustration

This example of how to calculate shareholder value starts with operating value driver assumptions and ends with shareholder value. The expectations investing process operates in reverse: It starts with market value and solves for the price-implied expectations. The mechanics are the same going in either direction.

Assume that last year's sales were $100 million and that you expect the following value drivers to be constant over an entire five-year forecast period:

Sales growth rate	10%
Operating profit margin	15%
Cash tax rate	25%
Incremental fixed-capital investment rate	15%
Incremental working-capital investment rate	10%
Cost of capital	8%

Assume that the company has no nonoperating assets or debt.

Shareholder value of $257.07 is the sum of the $47.44 million cumulative present value of free cash flow in the forecast period and the $209.63 million present value of continuing value (see table 2.1).[20] In this illustration we used the perpetuity-with-inflation method and an assumed rate of inflation of 2 percent.

Table 2.1
Summary illustration

	Year 1	Year 2	Year 3	Year 4	Year 5
Sales	$110.00	$121.00	$133.10	$146.41	$161.05
Operating profit	16.50	18.15	19.97	21.96	24.16
Less: Cash taxes on operating profit	4.13	4.54	4.99	5.49	6.04
Net operating profit after taxes (NOPAT)	12.38	13.61	14.97	16.47	18.12
Fixed-capital investment	1.50	1.65	1.82	2.00	2.20
Working-capital investment	1.00	1.10	1.21	1.33	1.46
Total investment	2.50	2.75	3.03	3.33	3.66
Free cash flow	9.88	10.86	11.95	13.14	14.46
Present value of free cash flow	9.14	9.31	9.49	9.66	9.84
Cumulative present value of free cash flow	9.14	18.46	27.94	37.60	47.44
Present value of continuing value					209.63
Shareholder value					$257.07

Essential Ideas

- The magnitude, timing, and riskiness of cash flows determine the market prices of financial assets, including bonds, real estate, and stocks.
- You can estimate the shareholder value of a stock by forecasting free cash flows and discounting them back to the present.
- Rather than struggle to forecast long-term cash flows or employ unreliable, short-term valuation proxies, expectations investors establish the future cash flow performance implied by stock prices as a benchmark for deciding whether to buy, hold, or sell.

Appendix: Estimating Continuing Value

Discounted cash flow valuation models commonly forecast cash flows in two parts: the expected cash flows during the explicit forecast period and the continuing value that captures the cash flows expected beyond the explicit forecast period.

There are significant assumptions packed into a continuing value calculation, so it is important that you have a clear sense of how reasonable they are. The key is to consider carefully what the company's competitive position will be at the end of the explicit forecast period.

There are three inputs for you to assess. The first is the cost of capital. You want to use a cost of capital that matches the company's expected competitive position after the explicit forecast period. This is particularly important for young companies because corporate risk, and therefore the cost of capital, often declines as companies mature.

Next is inflation. The question is whether the company will be able to preserve purchasing power by pricing its goods or services in line with inflation. Companies in stable industries with low price elasticity of demand are best positioned to keep up with inflation. Price elasticity measures how much demand changes with changes in price. Goods and services with low price elasticity see stable demand even as prices rise.

Finally, you should consider the possibility of growth beyond the explicit forecast period. There may be the rare company that can maintain purchasing power and grow above and beyond inflation. At the other end of the spectrum, negative growth comes into play for declining industries. Most companies fall somewhere in between those extremes.

Note the interaction between the continuing value method you select and the market-implied forecast period. The more value you assign to continuing value, the less the value that will be allocated to the explicit forecast period. A proper approach to the continuing value is therefore essential to an accurate portrayal of market expectations.

We recommend that you estimate continuing value with the perpetuity, perpetuity-with-inflation, perpetuity-with-partial-inflation, or perpetuity-with-decline approach. Here's a quick discussion of each.

The Perpetuity Method

The perpetuity method assumes that a company generating returns greater than its cost of capital will attract competition that will drive returns on new investments down to the cost of capital by the end of the forecast period. Even if a company grows beyond the forecast period, it will create no further value because it will earn a return on its investments equal only to the cost of capital. You can capture this dynamic by treating all cash flows after the forecast period as a perpetual stream of identical cash flows. The perpetuity method simplifies the calculation greatly because we don't need to discount individual cash flows.[21]

To determine the present value of a perpetuity, simply divide the expected annual cash flow at the end of the forecast period by the rate of return:

Equation 2.5:

$$\text{Present value of a perpetuity} = \frac{\text{Annual cash flow}}{\text{Rate of return}}$$

Using the perpetuity method, we calculate the present value at the end of the forecast period by dividing NOPAT, or free cash flow before incremental investment, by the cost of capital:

Equation 2.6:

$$\text{Perpetuity continuing value} = \frac{\text{NOPAT}}{\text{Cost of capital}}$$

NOPAT, not free cash flow, is the correct perpetuity because the present value of the incremental investment outlays is offset exactly by the expected present value of the incremental cash inflows.

Since investments made after the forecast period do not affect value, the continuing value calculation has to account only for enough investment to maintain existing capacity. The perpetuity method assumes that depreciation expense approximates the cost of maintaining existing capacity. That is another reason that NOPAT is the numerator.

To illustrate, let's say that the cost of capital is 8 percent and NOPAT for the last year of the forecast period is $1.00. The continuing value using the perpetuity method (equation 2.6) is simply the $1.00 NOPAT divided by the 8 percent cost of capital, or $12.50.

The perpetuity method assumes that while a business earns the cost of capital in the post-forecast period, its cash flow growth does not keep up with the rate of inflation.

The Perpetuity-with-Inflation Method

Unlike the perpetuity method, the perpetuity-with-inflation approach assumes that the cash flows will grow annually at the inflation rate in the post-forecast period. The formula for the present value at the end of the forecast period is an algebraic simplification of a growing perpetuity.

Equation 2.7:

$$\text{Perpetuity with inflation} = \frac{\text{NOPAT} \times (1 + \text{Inflation rate})}{(\text{Cost of capital} - \text{Inflation rate})}$$

How do the perpetuity and perpetuity-with-inflation methods differ? In both approaches the cost of capital includes expected inflation. However, the cash flow in the numerator of the perpetuity model provides for no increases at the inflation rate. Future cash flows are constant in nominal terms, but their value decreases each year after an adjustment for inflation. In contrast, cash flows in the perpetuity-with-inflation model grow each year at the anticipated inflation rate. They therefore keep up with inflation and are hence constant in real terms. Predictably, when we anticipate inflation, the perpetuity-with-inflation model produces higher values than does the perpetuity model.

For instance, say we use the same assumptions as above but now introduce an expected inflation rate of 2 percent. In the perpetuity-with-inflation method (equation 2.7), NOPAT increases by the inflation rate, to $1.02. Divide $1.02 by 6 percent (8 percent cost of capital minus 2 percent expected inflation) to yield a continuing value of $17.00.[22]

In the rare case that you expect a company to not only match the rate of inflation but also grow above and beyond it, you can substitute a growth term for inflation. This will generate a higher continuing value than will the perpetuity-with-inflation method.

But this scenario is sufficiently rare that we recommend using it very sparingly.

The Perpetuity-with-Partial-Inflation Method

The perpetuity-with-partial-inflation approach assumes that the perpetuity will grow annually in the post-forecast period at the rate greater than zero but less than the full inflation rate. The formula is the same as a growth in perpetuity with an additional variable, *p*, that reflects the percentage of inflation the company will be able to recoup.

Equation 2.8:

$$\text{Perpetuity with partial-inflation} = \frac{\text{NOPAT} \times \left[1 + (p \times \text{Inflation rate}) \right]}{(\text{Cost of capital} - [p \times \text{Inflation rate}])}$$

Let's stay with our example of a cost of capital of 8 percent, expected inflation of 2 percent, and NOPAT in the last year of the forecast period of $1.00. Now assume that the company can price its goods or services into perpetuity at one-half the rate of inflation. The variable *p* would therefore equal 0.5.

In this case, the numerator would be $1.01 ($1.00 of NOPAT times one-half of the inflation rate) and the denominator would be 7 percent (8 percent cost of capital minus one-half of 2 percent expected inflation). The perpetuity-with-partial-inflation method (equation 2.8) yields a value of $14.43 ($1.01 divided by 7 percent).

The Perpetuity-with-Decline Method

Most businesses eventually go into decline at some point. Examples include video rental services, printed newspapers, and photography film. If you expect a business to be in decline at the end of the forecast period, you can conveniently use the same formula as perpetuity-with-inflation but replace the inflation term with one for the rate of decline.

Equation 2.9:

$$\text{Perpetuity with decline} = \frac{\text{NOPAT} \times (1 - \text{Decline})}{(\text{Cost of capital} + \text{Decline})}$$

Let's say an industry is expected to decline at a 2 percent rate, NOPAT for the last year of the forecast period is $1.00, and the cost of capital is 8 percent. Divide $0.98 ($1.00 × 0.98) by 10 percent (8 percent cost of capital plus the 2 percent decline rate) to yield a continuing value of $9.80.

Which model is right for you? There is no easy answer. Think about inflation and growth in the context of the industry in which the company competes. Factors to consider include barriers to entry and the risk of disruptive innovation. We discuss these topics in chapter 4. In practice, we believe the perpetuity-with-partial-inflation method is most appropriate for most companies.

3

The Expectations Infrastructure

EXPECTATIONS INVESTING is based on two simple ideas: First, you can read stock prices and estimate the expectations that they imply. Second, you will earn superior returns only if you correctly anticipate revisions in those price-implied expectations.

We use the discounted cash flow model to read expectations because that's how the market values stocks. Price-implied expectations can be expressed using familiar operating value drivers, including sales growth, operating profit margin, and investment.

We now turn to expectations revisions and deal with two fundamental questions:

1. Where should we look for expectations revisions?
2. Are all expectations revisions created equally?

The answers are vital because they hold the key to earning attractive investment returns. Knowing today's expectations is one thing, but it is another thing altogether to know what they will be and the impact they will have on shareholder value. Let's start with the first question.

The Expectations Infrastructure

The operating value drivers are a logical place to start the search for expectations revisions. Indeed, investors and managers typically create ranges around each of the value drivers to test how various outcomes affect shareholder value. We too advocated this sensitivity analysis until we realized that the method doesn't truly capture the underpinnings of expectations revisions.

To see why, take a simple example. Let's say that the price-implied expectation for a company's operating profit margin is 15 percent. A sensitivity analysis substitutes a range of margins, for instance from 12 to 18 percent, for the 15 percent and measures the impact on shareholder value. But any change in the operating margin assumption raises larger questions: Why will margins change from current expectations? Will a change in sales growth expectations precipitate it? Or will the company modify its cost structure more aggressively than investors currently contemplate? We know there is more to the story since value drivers change for many reasons.

To understand expectations revisions, we must realize that changes in operating value drivers are really the culminating effect, not the fundamental cause, of expectations revisions. It turns out that the right place for expectations revisions is with the fundamental building blocks of shareholder value: sales, operating costs, and investments. We call them value triggers because they start the expectations revisions process. Importantly, investors and managers think and talk in precisely these terms.

But the problem is that value triggers are too broad to be mapped directly to the operating value drivers. For example, an increase in a company's expected sales may or may not cause operating profit margins to change. We need one more set of analytical tools to systematically capture the relationship between the value triggers and the value drivers. We call them the value factors. They include volume, price and mix, operating leverage, economies of scale, cost efficiencies, and investment efficiencies.

Value triggers, value factors, and operating value drivers constitute the expectations infrastructure (figure 3.1). We now know where to begin to look for revisions in expectations: the value triggers. Once we've identified a potential change, we consider which value factors come into play. Finally, we can translate the

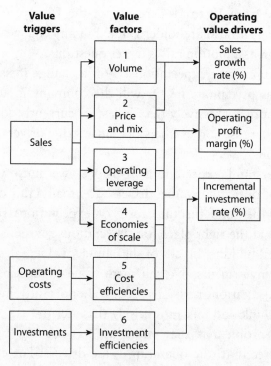

FIGURE 3.1 The expectations infrastructure.

revisions into value driver terms and calculate their impact on shareholder value.

The expectations infrastructure is based on established microeconomic principles and guides rigorous analysis of historical and prospective performance. It also sorts out cause and effect, providing investors with a clear means to evaluate all the factors that come into play with a trigger revision. Most Wall Street investors who use sensitivity analysis fail to capture these dynamics.

Let's go to the core of the expectations infrastructure and discuss each of the value factors.

Value Factor 1: Volume

Changes in volume, price, and sales mix assumptions lead to revisions in sales growth expectations. Specifically, volume captures the expectations revisions for how many units of a good or service are sold. Volume changes clearly induce sales changes and may also affect operating profit margins. We need to focus only on the sales impact here since we capture the margin effects via two additional factors, operating leverage and economies of scale.

Value Factor 2: Price and Mix

Changes in selling prices and sales mix affect both the sales growth rate and the operating profit margin. A change in selling price means that a company sells the same unit at a different price. You need to consider a company's costs in conjunction with price changes in order to assess the impact on operating profit margins.

Sales mix reflects a change in the distribution of high- and low-margin products. Whether operating profit margins expand or contract depends on how the mix changes.

Goodyear Tire & Rubber is a good example of how sales mix can improve operating profit margins. Goodyear's sales in 2015 were 28 percent lower than those in 2011, and its total unit volume was down 8 percent. Yet the company's operating profit rose nearly 50 percent over that period, and its operating profit margin expanded 6 percentage points. The key was a shift in mix from low-margin commodity tires to high-margin premium tires.[1]

Value Factor 3: Operating Leverage

Businesses invariably spend significant amounts of money before their products and services generate sales. These outlays are called preproduction costs. Some businesses, such as utilities and chemical companies, spend primarily on physical facilities and equipment that they record on their balance sheets and expense, via depreciation, over the estimated useful lives of the assets. Other businesses, including software and pharmaceutical companies, immediately expense their significant knowledge development costs but don't spend much on depreciable assets. The relative significance of preproduction costs and the time required to develop products or services varies across industries and companies.

Preproduction outlays dampen operating profit margins. Subsequent sales growth, on the other hand, leads to higher operating profit margins. Investors and managers commonly call this operating leverage.

The timing and magnitude of preproduction costs differ by business. Companies that rely on physical capital need a new round of preproduction costs to sustain growth as they approach their practical capacity utilization. These new costs place downward pressure on margins. In contrast, knowledge companies worry relatively little about their physical capacity. But to avoid obsolescence, they must incur successive rounds of product development costs in order to upgrade existing products and introduce new products.

Table 3.1
Operating leverage

	Year 0	Year 1	Year 2
Sales	$100.00	$110.00	$121.00
Preproduction costs	17.00	17.00	17.00
Other operating expenses (68% of sales)	68.00	74.80	82.28
Total operating costs	85.00	91.80	99.28
Operating profit	$15.00	$18.20	$21.72
Operating profit margin	15.00%	16.55%	17.95%

So how exactly does operating leverage affect operating profit margin? Assume that a company had sales of $100 million and pretax operating profit of $15 million in the most recent year. Further assume that preproduction costs accounted for 20 percent, or $17 million, of the $85 million in operating costs. Because the company completed a major expansion last year, preproduction costs remain flat over the next two years while other operating costs continue at 68 percent of sales.

We can use these assumptions to calculate the operating profit for the first two forecast years (table 3.1).

Operating leverage increases the operating profit margin from 15 percent in the base year to 16.55 percent and 17.95 percent in years 1 and 2, respectively.

Value Factor 4: Economies of Scale

Economies of scale exist when a business can perform essential tasks, such as purchasing, production, marketing, sales, distribution, and customer service, at a lower cost per unit as volume increases.

One example is "swipe fees," the percentage of a transaction that banks charge retailers each time a customer swipes a credit card to make a purchase. Large merchants such as Walmart Inc., Costco Wholesale Corp., and Amazon.com Inc. use their size to negotiate lower fees than what smaller retailers pay.[2] Big companies also enjoy economies of scale in advertising because higher volume enables them not only to negotiate lower prices but also to reach more potential customers. These scale economies give larger companies a cost advantage over smaller competitors and can deter new competitors from entering the marketplace if they are sufficiently significant.

The simple pursuit of market share and scale is no panacea. For example, Southwest Airlines and steel producer Nucor developed superior business models and became more profitable than their much larger competitors. Also, companies focused on volume growth may struggle to change course with the market in industries with rapid technological change and shifting customer demands. Too often, market leaders fall prey not only to costly bureaucracy but also to hubris.

That said, more than three-quarters of U.S. industries are more concentrated today than they were in the late 1990s as a consequence of substantial merger activity. This has led to higher operating profit margins for the industries that are most concentrated.[3]

Note that economies of scale differ from operating leverage.[4] Whereas economies of scale generate greater efficiency as volumes increase, operating leverage is the result of spreading preproduction costs over larger volumes. Mistaking economies of scale for operating leverage may lead you to falsely conclude that a company's unit costs will continue to fall even as it expands capacity to meet demand.

The importance of economies of scale to expectations investors depends not on the magnitude of a company's past scale economies but rather on the extent to which the market's current expectations fail to reflect plausible changes.[5]

Value Factor 5: Cost Efficiencies

Cost efficiencies that are unrelated to scale can also affect operating profit margin. These efficiencies span activities from the acquisition of raw materials to the sale and distribution of goods or services. Companies achieve cost efficiencies in two fundamental ways.[6] Either they reduce costs within activities, or they significantly reconfigure their activities.

Chiquita Brands International, which distributes bananas and other produce, is an example of a company that has enjoyed cost efficiencies. With more than twenty thousand employees, managing human resources is a major task. In recent years, the company adopted new human capital management software that allowed it to reduce its costs in this vital activity by 30 percent.[7]

Reconfiguring purchasing, production, sales, marketing, or distribution activities can dramatically shift a company's cost position. Apple Inc., which designs, develops, and sells consumer electronics, is a case in point. Apple started as a personal computer company, and in the 1980s it built its computers in the United States. The company's most successful product is now the iPhone. Apple has developed a global supply chain since the phone's launch in 2007. Components come from suppliers all over the world, and the assembly of iPhones has shifted predominately to China. Outsourcing activities that did not create value enabled Apple to lower its costs and capture more of the overall value created by the iPhone.[8] Here again, the focus should not be on the size of cost savings, but on the savings potential beyond the market's current expectations.

Value Factor 6: Investment Efficiencies

Businesses enjoy investment efficiencies when they can invest less for a given level of sales and operating profit.[9] For example, McDonald's continues to grow by opening new stores. In the 1990s, the company figured out a way to minimize new store investment, including the building itself, the land, and the equipment. In 1990, the average cost for a traditional McDonald's restaurant was $1.6 million. By 1994, McDonald's had trimmed the cost to $1.1 million by simplifying the building design and using modular buildings, which require smaller land parcels. The company also standardized its equipment, which allowed it to source globally and to demand lower prices from its main suppliers. The new stores generated the same sales and operating profits as the old ones, but the cost to build them was 30 percent lower.

Mondelez International, a multinational food and beverage company, has benefited from another form of investment efficiency, an improving cash conversion cycle. The cash conversion cycle measures how many days it takes for a company to convert its investments in inventory and other resources into cash flows from sales. From 2013 to 2020, Mondelez improved its cycle from 39 days to −35 days, which means that it now collects cash before it pays its suppliers. Mondelez's working-capital efficiency freed more than $3.6 billion in capital.

Not All Expectations Revisions Are Equal

The expectations infrastructure provides a detailed map of what's behind sales, operating profit margin, and investments. It also shows why we need to start with the value triggers to maximize our chances of successfully anticipating revisions in expectations. But we still have to answer the question of whether all expectations revisions are equal. The answer is an unequivocal no. To see why, consider two related questions:

1. Which expectations changes are likely to offer investors the best opportunities: sales, costs, or investments?
2. When do these changes really matter?

The first question has a clear answer: Changes in sales expectations are the most likely to present attractive investment opportunities. Why? Take another look at the expectations infrastructure (figure 3.1). Note that sales trigger four of the six value factors. That alone is compelling, but we also need to consider that revisions in expectations for sales growth are typically the largest. Revisions in expectations due to cost and investment efficiencies are almost always smaller. But even the magnitude of the value driver shifts does not tell the whole story, because our primary interest is the impact on shareholder value.

The degree to which changes in sales growth expectations matter depends on whether a company is creating shareholder value. Sales growth adds value when a company generates returns on its growth investments that exceed its cost of capital. If returns fall below the cost of capital, then growth destroys value. Finally, if a company earns exactly the cost of capital, growth adds no value. Growth can be good news, bad news, or no news.

A company adds value when the present value of incremental net operating profit after taxes (NOPAT) exceeds incremental investment. NOPAT growth, in turn, depends on the expected sales growth rate, operating profit margin, and assumed cash tax rate. So the operating profit margin determines the impact on shareholder value added for a given change in expectations for sales growth.[10] The higher the margin, the better. However, a company needs to earn a certain break-even operating profit margin, which we call the threshold margin, just to maintain its value.[11]

To illustrate the threshold margin, we return to the summary illustration from chapter 2. Last year's sales were $100 million, and NOPAT was $11.25. Let's assume a one-year forecast period with the following market expectations:

Sales growth rate	10%
Operating profit margin	15%
Cash tax rate	25%
Incremental investment rate	25%

The company's cost of capital is 8 percent, the expected inflation rate is 2 percent, and we used the perpetuity-with-inflation method to calculate the continuing value (see equation 2.7). We calculate the shareholder value added of $12.69 for this set of assumptions in the column labeled "Operating profit margin of 15%" in table 3.2. In the column to the right, we substitute the 14.08 percent threshold margin for the 15 percent operating profit margin and shareholder value added drops to zero.[12]

The threshold margin reveals four principles that can help you determine when expectations changes affect shareholder value:

1. If expectations for the operating profit margin are well above the threshold margin, upward revisions in sales growth expectations will produce large increases in shareholder value. The larger the changes, the greater the increases.

2. If expectations for the operating profit margin are close to the threshold margin, then revisions in sales growth expectations produce relatively small increases in shareholder value. The exception is if the revisions also trigger higher margin expectations via revisions in sales mix, operating leverage, or economies of scale.

3. If expectations for the operating profit margin are significantly below the threshold margin, then positive revisions

Table 3.2
Shareholder value added: expectations versus threshold margin

	Year 0	Operating profit margin of 15%, year 1	Operating profit margin of 14.08%, year 1
Sales	$100.00	$110.00	$110.00
Operating profit	15.00	16.50	15.49
Less: Cash taxes	3.75	4.13	3.87
Net operating profit after taxes (NOPAT)	11.25	12.38	11.61
Less: Incremental investment		2.50	2.50
Free cash flow		9.88	9.11
Present value of free cash flow		9.14	8.44
Present value of continuing value	191.25	194.79	182.81
Shareholder value	$191.25	$203.94	$191.25
Shareholder value added		$12.69	$0.00

in sales growth expectations reduce shareholder value unless there are offsetting improvements in the operating profit margin or the investment rate.

4. A rise in expectations in the incremental investment rate increases the threshold margin and thereby reduces the value that sales growth adds. Similarly, a lower incremental investment rate translates into a lower threshold margin.

The wider the expected spread between operating profit margin and threshold margin and the faster the sales growth rate, the more likely it is that sales growth is the dominant trigger. The likelihood rises even more when changes in sales also trigger the other value factors, including price and mix, operating leverage, and economies of scale.

Revisions in sales expectations are insignificant for companies that earn returns close to the cost of capital and don't benefit much from price and mix, operating leverage, or economies of scale. In these cases, changes in cost or investment efficiency can contribute most to changes in shareholder value even if the absolute impact on shareholder value is small.

When expectations change, the expectations infrastructure helps you identify the potential sources of shareholder value added. The value triggers linked to the six value factors and the resulting operating value drivers are the analytical foundation for expectations investing analysis (see chapters 5 through 7).

The next chapter, the final chapter of part I, addresses the competitive issues that affect the fundamental value triggers. With the last piece in place, you will have all the strategic and financial tools you need to implement expectations investing.

Essential Ideas

- To earn superior returns, you must improve your odds of correctly anticipating revisions in market expectations.
- The expectations infrastructure is based on the fundamental value triggers, value factors, and operating value drivers that determine shareholder value. The infrastructure will help you visualize the causes and the effects of expectations revisions.
- Revisions in sales growth expectations are your most likely source of investment opportunities, but only when a company earns above the cost of capital on its investments.

4

Analyzing Competitive Strategy

COMPETITIVE STRATEGY analysis lies at the heart of security analysis. The surest way for investors to benefit from expectations revisions is to anticipate shifts in a company's competitive dynamics. These shifts lead to a revised outlook for sales, costs, or investments, the value triggers that initiate the expectations investing process. For investors, competitive strategy analysis is an essential tool for identifying the likely direction of expectations revisions.[1]

The Dual Uses of Competitive Strategy Analysis

The competitive strategy literature focuses largely on prescriptions for management action. But investors can use the same strategic tools in a different way.

Management's objective is to create value by making investments that earn a return in excess of the cost of capital. Indeed, sustainable value creation is the signature of competitive advantage. A company uses competitive strategy analysis for planning and decision making because its competitive advantage hinges squarely on the quality and execution of its strategy.

Investors play a different game. They generate superior returns when they correctly anticipate revisions in the market's expectations for a company's performance. Investors do not earn high rates of return on the stocks of the best value-creating companies if those stocks are priced to fully reflect that future performance. That is why great companies are not necessarily great stocks. An investor uses competitive strategy analysis as a means to anticipate revisions in expectations.

Historical Analysis

Looking at a company's historical results can give you a sense of what to anticipate. For one thing, you can see which operating value drivers have been most variable. You can then analyze this information, using the expectations infrastructure and competitive strategy analysis, to track the sources of that variability. History also provides you with a reality check. If the market expects a specific operating value driver to perform as it has in the past, you must have a good reason to believe that an expectations revision is likely.

The powerful combination of the expectations infrastructure and competitive strategy analysis highlights the economic and strategic factors that influence the operating value drivers. For example, a company may pass on cost savings to its customers through lower prices in order to accelerate unit volume growth. So even though lower prices offset the margin benefit of cost savings, price cuts are important because of their impact on sales growth. The expectations infrastructure provides a framework to assess cause and effect, whereas competitive strategy analysis goes beyond the numbers to assess a company's competitive circumstances. Table 4.1 presents some key issues, along with the

Table 4.1
Operating value drivers, value factors, and competitive strategy analysis

Operating value driver	Value factor	Key issues
Sales growth rate	Volume	• Industry growth • Market share • Customer retention (churn)
	Price and mix	• Price changes • Mix changes
Operating profit margin	Price and mix	• Price changes • Mix changes
	Operating leverage	• Preproduction costs • Position in investment cycle • Divisibility of investment
	Economies of scale	• Purchasing • Production • Distribution • Learning curve
	Cost efficiencies	• Process reconfiguration • Technology • Outsourcing
Incremental investment rate	Investment efficiencies	• Technology • Facilities reconfiguration • Working-capital management

operating value drivers and value factors, that you may want to consider when you evaluate historical results.

Naturally, the relevance of historical analysis varies from company to company. Its relative importance is largely a function of the availability of historical data and industry stability. In general, the more historical data available, the better. A long string of past results provides important insights about previous industry cycles, competitive clashes, and the effectiveness of management strategies.

Industry stability speaks to the reliability of historical value drivers. For stable industries, the future will likely look a great deal like the past, making a record of historical performance invaluable. In contrast, looking at the past performance of rapidly changing sectors or companies that compete in brand-new industries has limited practical value.

Framework for Assessing Competitive Strategy

We have found it useful to assess competitive advantage at three levels. First is getting the lay of the land by understanding the high-level characteristics of the industry. Next, you can do specific industry analysis. Industry attractiveness combines the market characteristics with an assessment of industry structure. Market characteristics include growth in the market, supply and demand fundamentals for both customers and suppliers, rate of innovation, and regulatory shifts. Industry structure involves market share, entry and exit barriers, vertical-integration potential, threat of substitute products, modes of competition, and industry profitability.

The final level of analysis seeks to identify firm-specific sources of advantage. An individual company generally has minimal influence over industry attractiveness. In contrast, the company's performance and competitive position are driven by its chosen strategies in areas such as product quality, technology, vertical integration, cost position, service, pricing, brand identification, and distribution channel focus. A company's strategic choices, in combination with its skills in execution, determine its prospects for creating value. We'll now touch on each level and offer some tools to guide the analysis.

Understanding the Industry Landscape

The goal of this level is to understand how the industry works and what some of its key traits are, including profitability, stability, and exposure to external forces. A good starting point is to create an industry map.[2] The objective is to understand the structure of competition and the elements that determine present and future profitability.

Start by putting the company you are analyzing in the middle of the map. It is common to have suppliers on the left and customers on the right. Try to include all companies that might have an impact on the profitability of the business. It is also helpful to list firms in order of size to get a sense of their relative positions. The boundaries of an industry are not always clear, but seeing where a company fits into a bigger picture helps draw out critical questions.

Creating a map also provides a good opportunity to think about the potential for new entrants. Consider which companies are not on the map now but are logical competitors in the future. The map also allows for an understanding of the nature of the economic interaction between companies. For example, are the relationships between entities contractual, based on best efforts, or pay as you go? Finally, evaluate other factors that may influence profitability, such as labor relations or geopolitical risks.

Figure 4.1 is an example of an industry map for the U.S. airline industry.

A value pool analysis allows you to see an industry's value creation.[3] The horizontal axis is a measure of size, such as sales or

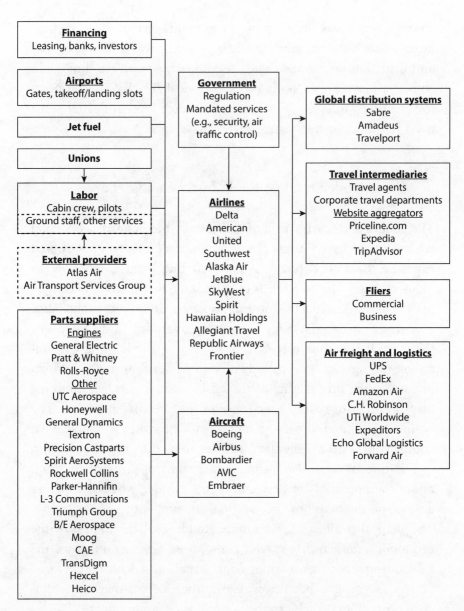

FIGURE 4.1 An industry map.

assets. The vertical axis reflects the spread between the operating profit margin and the threshold margin. Recall that threshold margin is the margin at which the company earns exactly the cost of capital. The value pool analysis tells you how big a company is and how much value it creates.

Figure 4.2 is an example of a value pool analysis for the U.S. airline industry in 2019. To really grasp the change in the nature of the industry, it is useful to do value pool analyses over time. In stable industries, the changes in value creation are modest from year to year, whereas substantial shifts in value suggest limited competitive advantages. Further, companies, especially large ones, that create substantial value are logical targets for competition.

The market share test provides a good measure of industry stability.[4] This analysis examines market share over two periods, typically three or five years apart, and calculates the average absolute change in market share. Table 4.2 provides an example for the global smartphone industry. The higher the average, the more

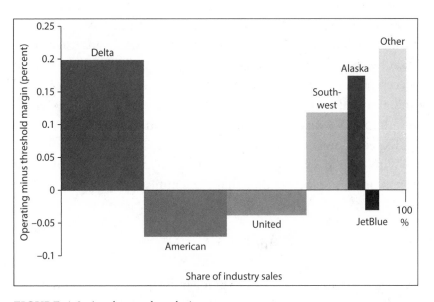

FIGURE 4.2 A value pool analysis.

Table 4.2
Market share test

Smartphones (global by units)	2014 (%)	2019 (%)	Five-year absolute change (%)
Samsung	24	20	4
Apple	15	13	2
Lenovo	7	3	4
Huawei	6	16	10
Xiaomi	5	8	3
LG	5	2	3
Others	38	38	0
Total	100	100	
Average absolute change			4

Source: Counterpoint Research.

market share is moving around and the less likely it is that any one of the companies has a sustainable competitive advantage.

Finally, it is critical to consider how external forces, including tariffs, subsidies, and regulations, might influence industry profitability. For instance, the stocks of U.S. steel producers rose in December 2019 when the United States restored tariffs on steel and aluminum imports from Brazil and Argentina, thereby reducing supply. We discuss this in more detail in chapter 12, "Sources of Expectations Opportunities."

With a solid sense of the industry landscape, we can turn our attention to the factors that shape the industry.

Industry Analysis

We suggest two frameworks to guide industry analysis, both developed by professors at Harvard Business School. First is Michael

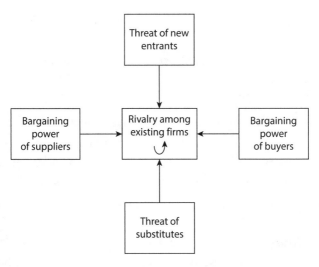

FIGURE 4.3 The five forces framework. From *Competitive Strategy: Techniques for Analyzing Industries and Competitors* by Michael E. Porter. Copyright © 1980 by The Free Press. Reprinted with the permission of The Free Press, a division of Simon & Schuster, Inc. All rights reserved.

Porter's well-known five forces framework, which helps define industry structure and is particularly useful for competitive analysis (figure 4.3).[5] Second is Clayton Christensen's model of disruptive innovation, which helps us anticipate the risk of companies failing.

Five Forces Framework

Industry structure is a major force in shaping the competitive rules of the game as well as the strategies available to competing firms. This analysis is applicable to most industries, but especially to those with the following three characteristics:

- *Defined boundaries.* You can readily define buyers, suppliers, and competitors.

- *Mature and relatively predictable patterns.* The industry is relatively stable.
- A *physical-capital orientation.* Physical assets are central to value creation.

Porter argues that the collective strength of the five forces determines an industry's potential for value creation. He stresses that although this potential varies from industry to industry, an individual company's strategies ultimately dictate its sustainable competitive advantage. Let's look at the five forces one by one:

- *Substitution threat* addresses the existence of substitute products or services, as well as the likelihood that a potential buyer will switch to a substitute product. A business faces a substitution threat if its prices are not competitive and if comparable products are available from competitors. Substitute products limit the prices that companies can charge, placing a ceiling on potential returns.
- *Buyer power* is the bargaining strength of the buyers of a product or service. It is a function of buyer concentration, switching costs, levels of information, substitute products, and the offering's importance to the buyer. Informed, large buyers have much more leverage over their suppliers than do uninformed, diffused buyers.
- *Supplier power* is the degree of leverage a supplier has with its customers in areas like price, quality, and service. An industry that cannot pass on price increases to its customers from its powerful suppliers is destined to be unattractive. Suppliers are well positioned if they are more concentrated than the industry they sell to, if they are not burdened by substitute products, or if their products have significant switching costs. They are also in a good position if the industry they serve represents a relatively small percentage of their sales volume or if the product is critical

to the buyer. Sellers of commodity goods to a concentrated number of buyers are in a much more difficult position than sellers of differentiated products to a diverse buyer base.

- *Barriers to entry* determine how difficult it is for a new competitor to enter an industry. These barriers might include the level of capital required, the strength of established brands and customer loyalty, access to distribution channels, economies of scale, the costs of switching from one supplier's product to another supplier's, and government regulations.

- *Rivalry among firms* addresses how fiercely companies compete with one another along dimensions such as price, service, warranties, new-product introductions, and advertising. Intense rivalry can make an industry unattractive for all participating companies. Factors that influence rivalry include industry growth, the relative size of preproduction costs, and the level of product differentiation. A growing industry tends to mitigate rivalry, as competitors often focus more on growing with the industry than on prevailing in zero-sum games. Industries with high preproduction costs usually exhibit significant rivalry, as there are strong incentives to drive sufficient volume to cover costs. Where little product differentiation exists, intense rivalry based on price and service frequently materializes.

Two of the forces, barriers to entry and rivalry, deserve additional discussion.

Competition is dynamic, so it is crucial to understand the pattern of entry and exit in the industry.[6] One starting point for assessing potential threats is an analysis of actual entries and exits. Young industries generally have more entry and exit than older industries do, but our experience suggests that entry and exit is more active in all industries than executives and investors commonly perceive.

A challenger's decision to enter an industry starts with an assessment of the expected response of the incumbents. Specific factors that predict the ferocity of incumbent reaction include asset specificity, the level of the minimum efficient production scale, excess capacity, and incumbent reputation.[7]

Economists used to believe that how much a company invested in its assets determined its reaction to challengers, but they came to realize that the key is how specific those assets are to the market. A firm whose assets are valuable only in a specific market will fight vigorously to maintain its position.

Examples of asset specificity include site specificity (a company locates assets next to a customer for efficiency), physical specificity (a company adapts assets to a specific transaction), dedicated assets (a company acquires assets to satisfy the needs of a particular buyer), and human specificity (a company provides specific skills or knowledge to its employees in order to target a particular business relationship).[8]

Unit costs decline as output rises in most industries. At some point, unit costs stop declining with incremental output and companies realize constant returns to scale. Minimum efficient scale is the smallest amount of production a company must achieve to minimize unit costs. It allows a challenger to figure out the size of its up-front investment and how much market share it needs to be competitive and create value.

The last two factors, excess capacity and incumbent reputation, are straightforward. If an industry has excess capacity, an entrant will add to that capacity and hence lead to lower prices. A firm's reputation as a fighter or as accommodating, backed by words and actions, will shape a potential entrant's decision.

An entrant must also assess the anticipated payoff of entering an industry because it won't be able to earn an attractive return if the incumbents have insurmountable advantages. These include precommitment contracts, licenses and patents, learning curve benefits, network effects, and the cost to exit.

Unique access to raw materials, long-term contracts with customers, and credible pledges to maintain the lowest prices in the industry are all examples of precommitment contracts. Licenses are costly and hence discourage entrance, while patents deter entry by protecting the incumbent's business for a specified period.

Network effects exist when the value of a good or service increases when more people use that good or service. Once one network becomes dominant, luring customers becomes difficult for a challenger. Classic examples include Microsoft's personal computer operating system, Facebook in social media, and Uber in ride sharing.

Entrants must weigh both their chances for success and the cost to exit. Exit barriers are a function of the magnitude of investment and the specificity of the acquired assets. Low investment needs and nonspecific assets are consistent with low barriers to entry and exit.

Rivalry among firms is the result of several factors, including the degree of cooperation, the homogeneity of objectives, demand variability, and industry growth.

In most industries there is a tension between *cooperating* and *cheating*. These terms come from game theory, which studies strategic interaction between two or more participants. Cooperation, which of course cannot be explicit in business, occurs when industry participants manage variables such as pricing and capacity additions in rough coordination. Cheating occurs when one firm lowers the price on its product or adds capacity when others don't in order to increase its proportion of industry profits. The heart of understanding rivalry is an assessment of each firm's perceived trade-off between cooperation and cheating. Lots of cooperation is consistent with minimal rivalry and attractive economic returns. Intense rivalry makes it difficult for firms to generate high returns.

The homogeneity of objectives of competitors is also essential to assess. Rivalry tends to be less intense in industries where companies have similar goals, time horizons, incentive programs, ownership structures, and corporate philosophies. This is rarely the case. For example, you can imagine an industry with companies that are public, privately held, or owned by private equity firms. Those competitors will have disparate financial objectives, time horizons, and incentive structures that may lead to different tactics and strategies.

The variability of demand for the industry's goods or services is also important. Companies struggle to coordinate internally, much less externally, when demand variability is high. Variable demand is especially relevant for industries with high fixed costs because of the risk of too much investment even at the peak level of demand. That excess capacity can lead to intense competition at the bottom of the cycle.

Companies can create shareholder value without undermining their competitors when an industry is growing rapidly. Stagnant industries are more similar to zero-sum games where the only way to increase value is to take it from others. Increased industry rivalry often accompanies decelerating industry growth.

Model of Disruptive Innovation

The late Clayton Christensen developed the model of disruptive innovation, which helps anticipate changes in expectations.[9] The model exposes a pattern by which dominant companies can fail, leading to sharply lowered expectations. This framework is particularly relevant for the following types of companies:

- *Market leaders.* These companies listen to their customers and focus on current profits. As a result, their inertia and incentives often cause them to miss significant technological shifts.
- *Organizationally centralized companies.* Companies that centralize their decision making often have difficulty seeing disruptive technologies emerge.

- *Companies that employ physical goods.* Incumbents can struggle as the products they sell transition from physical to digital.

Christensen argues that many companies lose their leadership positions even though great managers are making sound decisions based on widely accepted management principles. Hence the dilemma. His framework is based on three findings:

First, sustaining technologies and disruptive technologies are quite distinct. Sustaining technologies foster product improvement. They can be incremental, discontinuous, or even radical. But sustaining technologies operate within a defined value network, which he defines as the "context within which a firm identifies and responds to customers' needs, solves problems, procures input, reacts to competitors, and strives for profit."[10] Disruptive technologies offer the market a very different value proposition.

Products based on disruptive technologies may initially appeal only to a relatively few customers who value features such as low price, smaller size, or greater convenience. Other disruptive technologies comprise a new or emerging market segment that industry incumbents do not serve. Christensen finds that disruptive technologies generally underperform established products in the near term. Thus, not surprisingly, leading companies often overlook, ignore, or dismiss disruptive technologies in the early phases of the technology.

Second, technologies often progress faster than the market demands. Established companies commonly provide customers with more than they need or more than they are ultimately willing to pay for. This allows disruptive technologies to emerge because even if they underperform the demands of many users today, the improvement in their performance makes them fully competitive tomorrow.

Finally, passing over disruptive technologies may appear rational for established companies because disruptive products generally offer low margins, operate in insignificant or emerging markets, and are not in demand by the company's most profitable customers. As a result, companies that listen to their customers and practice conventional financial discipline are apt to pass on disruptive technologies.

Certainly, companies should not stop listening to their customers. Rather, companies must both meet the needs of their customers today and anticipate their needs for tomorrow. Sometimes customers themselves don't know which products or services they will want. Given that disruptive technologies may provide solutions to tomorrow's customers, companies must always balance what works now and what might work in the future because today's solutions may quickly become obsolete. As Andy Grove, the legendary CEO of Intel, put it, "Only the paranoid survive."[11]

The movie rental business is an example of a disruptive technology in action.[12] In the late 1990s, Blockbuster Video was a leader in movie rentals for home viewing. In the early 2000s, the company operated more than nine thousand stores and had a market capitalization of $5 billion. Blockbuster allowed customers to rent a movie for a specific period, after which it would charge a late fee. It is reported that Blockbuster earned $800 million in late fees in one year alone, more than 15 percent of the company's revenue.[13]

Netflix was founded in 1997 and improved the customer proposition along several important dimensions, including convenience by shipping DVDs and imposing no late fees. Netflix introduced streaming in 2007, removing the need to deal with physical discs, and eventually started producing its own content. Netflix completely redefined the game and launched a new value network. As of 2020, Netflix had a market capitalization of $200 billion, while Blockbuster filed for bankruptcy in 2010.

Disruptive technologies cause investors to lower expectations for some well-known companies while new and valuable companies are created. For example, makers of laptop computers were

ANTICIPATING COMPETITOR MOVES

> If you're thinking about building a new paper facility, you're going to base your decision on some assumptions about economic growth. . . . *What we never seem to factor in, however, is the response of our competitors. Who else is going to build a plant or machine at the same time?*
> —CFO, INTERNATIONAL PAPER (EMPHASIS ADDED)*

You can't assess a company's actions in a void because companies respond to each other's competitive moves. Game theory is a useful tool for thinking about industry rivalry and is particularly applicable in two business situations: pricing and capacity additions in a cyclical business.†

Industries that price their products cooperatively garner greater industry profits than those that compete on price. This was shown by an exchange between two Chinese taxi-hailing companies, Kuadi Dache, controlled by Alibaba, and Didi Dache, partially owned by Tencent. In early 2014, Didi Dache cut fares and introduced subsidies in an effort to gain market share. Kuadi Dache matched the actions immediately. Industry profits tumbled as the competitors spent $325 million in less than six months. The firms relented in June of that year with relative market shares similar to what they were before the price war. The companies ended up merging in 2015, which helped rationalize the market further.††

Another illustration is the decision to add capacity at a cyclical peak. If a company adds capacity and its competitors do not, it earns significant incremental profits. If it forgoes the investment and its competitors add the capacity, the competitors earn the incremental profits. If all the players add capacity, however, no one benefits and the next cyclical downturn is more painful for all. Thus the competitive reactions to a company's actions can have a material impact on expectations revisions.

---

* "Stern Stewart EVA Roundtable," *Journal of Applied Corporate Finance* 7, no. 4 (Summer 1994): 46–70.
† Adam M. Brandenburger and Barry J. Nalebuff, *Co-opetition*: 1. *A Revolutionary Mindset That Combines Competition and Cooperation*. 2. *The Game Theory Strategy That's Changing the Game of Business* (New York: Doubleday, 1996).
†† Charles Clover, "China's Internet Giants End Expensive Taxi App Wars," *Financial Times*, August 17, 2014.

disrupted by the introduction of the smartphone. You should be alert for the emergence of new value networks and the seeds of changes in expectations that they sow.

The five forces analysis is a valuable way to understand the drivers of profitability at the industry level, and the disruptive innovation framework is useful to assess threats to the status quo. But we ultimately want to understand potential expectations revisions for individual companies. For that we need to turn to an assessment of a firm's relative position.

How Companies Add Value

Adam Brandenburger and Harborne Stuart, professors of strategy, offer a very concrete and sound definition of how a firm adds value.[14] Their equation is simple.

Equation 4.1:

$$\text{Value created} = \text{Willingness to pay} - \text{Opportunity cost}$$

It says that the value a company creates is the difference between what it gets for its product or service and what it costs to produce that product (including the opportunity cost of capital).

Some definitions are useful here. Let's start with willingness to pay. Imagine that someone hands you a new tennis racket. Since you enjoy tennis, that is valuable to you. Now imagine that the same person slowly withdraws small amounts of money from your bank account. The amount of money at which you are indifferent between having the racket or the cash is your willingness to pay. You enjoy a consumer surplus if you can buy a product or service for less than your willingness to pay.

Opportunity cost is simply the flip side. You go to a store and take a tennis racket off the shelf. Opportunity cost is the amount of cash the store needs from you to make it indifferent between having the money or the racket.

This leads to the two main ways a company can create value. The first is to be able to increase the willingness to pay of customers while remaining competitive on costs. That strategy is generally called differentiation. When you hear differentiation, you should think of the ability to charge a higher relative price.

The second is the ability to produce a good or service at a lower relative cost while being able to charge a sufficient price. This is a low-cost strategy. The cost advantage may be the result of lower operating costs or more efficient use of capital. Indeed, many disruptive innovations succeed through lower costs and capital needs. Figure 4.4 summarizes these strategic positions and includes the rare company that enjoys above-average customer willingness to pay and below-average costs.

Now that we know how companies can add value to enjoy a competitive advantage, we need to isolate the source of the superior performance. For this, we return to the work of Michael Porter.

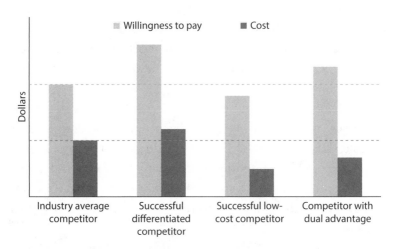

FIGURE 4.4 Sources of value. From Pankaj Ghemawat, *Strategy and the Business Landscape*, 4th ed. (New York: Ghemawat Publishing, 2017), 51. Used by permission of the author.

Value Chain Analysis

Michael Porter popularized value chain analysis, which views a business as a "collection of activities that are performed to design, produce, market, deliver, and support its product."[15] Joan Magretta, a scholar and editor who has worked closely with Porter and has provided an excellent exposition of his work, writes that "*activities* are discrete economic functions or processes, such as managing a supply chain, operating a sales force, developing products, or delivering them to the customer."[16]

Porter and Magretta argue that you cannot understand competitive advantage by looking at functional areas or at the firm as a whole. Rather, you must analyze the discrete activities that a company performs to deliver its goods or services. Each activity contributes or detracts from a company's ability to capture and sustain competitive advantage.

Porter shows that you can analyze a company's cost position or product differentiation relative to its peers by disaggregating its strategically relevant activities. A comparison of value chains among companies within an industry helps you see the points of difference that determine competitive advantage.

Value chain analysis is relevant for most businesses, but especially those engaging in two key types of activities:

- *Vertically integrated activities.* Vertically integrated businesses engage in all the activities necessary to convert raw materials into a final product. Value chain analysis helps identify which activities a company performs relatively efficiently. This analysis is especially useful when a company can substantially improve or outsource low-return activities.
- *Activities susceptible to technological change.* Technology causes value chains to disintegrate and allows companies to specialize in a narrow set of activities. Vertically

integrated companies that rely on a handful of activities for their profitability are at risk from specialized companies that perform a specific activity better.

Figure 4.5 shows the value chain, which allows you to disaggregate the activities of a firm into strategically relevant parts and to assess how the firm's activities compare to those of other industry participants.

Magretta suggests some ways to use the value chain to pinpoint a company's potential sources of competitive advantage:

- *Compare the company to the industry.* See how the configuration of activities compares to the industry. Look for points of difference that may reflect a competitive advantage or disadvantage. A company with a value chain that closely resembles its peers is likely engaged in what Michael Porter calls a "competition to be the best," a path to poor performance.
- *Identify the drivers of price or sources of differentiation.* To create superior value, a company needs to perform activities differently or to perform different activities. This requires trade-offs, where going down one strategic fork in the road precludes following the other. Differences can come anywhere along the value chain.
- *Identify the drivers of cost.* Estimate the costs associated with each activity. Look for differences between the cost structure of the company and that of its competitors. You

FIGURE 4.5 The value chain. From Joan Magretta, *Understanding Michael Porter: The Essential Guide to Competition and Strategy* (Boston, MA: Harvard Business Review Press, 2012), 76. Used by permission.

can gain crucial insights by pinpointing the specific drivers of a cost advantage or disadvantage.

Value chain thinking, Magretta suggests, leads to some important consequences. The first is that activities are no longer viewed solely as costs but as steps that add value to the end good or service. This allows you to match the value chain to what creates value for customers. The second is that this analysis compels a look beyond the firm to include a larger value system that includes other entities. For instance, e-commerce companies such as Amazon.com rely on the ability to deliver products on time. They need to execute activities to make sure that the shippers they rely on for delivery get the job done.

At this point, your analysis should have provided you with a sense of what the industry looks like, the drivers of profitability and risks of disruption, and the potential sources of competitive advantage for the company you are studying. This assessment forms a basis for determining whether a company is likely to meet, miss, or beat the expectations for financial performance implied by its stock price.

Information Economics

In recent decades, the primary form of investment for many companies has shifted from tangible to intangible assets. This affects how investments are represented in financial statements and requires understanding distinctions between physical and knowledge goods. In their book, *Information Rules*, the economists Carl Shapiro and Hal Varian convincingly show that basic economic principles are durable enough to explain the information economy.[17] The key is that companies based on knowledge assets have characteristics that are distinct from companies based on physical assets. As a result, you must evaluate them somewhat differently.

In this section, we highlight some of these characteristics and share two models that we have found useful. In almost all cases, these models are consistent with frameworks we have explored earlier. Here are some attributes of information goods worth considering:

- *High up-front costs, low incremental costs.* Many knowledge products are very costly to create the first time. Once in digital form, however, they are relatively inexpensive to replicate and distribute. Take software. Microsoft spends billions of dollars annually on research and development. But replicating and distributing that software is extremely cheap. As a result, Microsoft has enjoyed "increasing returns."[18] Virtually every dollar of revenue from each additional product sale increases the earnings and cash flow for a knowledge company. Thus, knowledge-based companies can enjoy increasing, not diminishing, returns for some period.

- *Network effects.* Network effects exist when the value of a product or service increases as more members use that product or service. As an example, Uber is a ride-hailing company that is attractive to riders and drivers precisely because so many riders and drivers congregate on the platform. In a particular category, positive feedback often means that one network becomes dominant. So as winner-take-all markets develop, variability increases as industry profits migrate to the dominant player. Expectations for the winner rise just as expectations for the losers deflate.

- *Lock-in.* Once customers develop user skills with a given product, or set corporate standards for a product, they often hesitate to switch to a competing offering, even if a rival product performs better or has a lower price. Hence, the company has "locked in" customers, making them more open to purchasing highly profitable product upgrades than they are to purchasing products from other sources. Shapiro and Varian cite multiple forms of lock-in, including brand-specific training and loyalty programs.[19]

The model we review next was created by Ben Thompson, the author of a newsletter focused on strategy in the technology industry called *Stratechery*. Thompson developed theories of aggregators and platforms, which can help explain the competitive positioning of companies in the technology and media industries. Here is a brief summary of those models:

- *Aggregation theory.* Aggregators are companies that consolidate abundant content from suppliers and make the content easily accessible for users. Google is a classic example. You search Google and it connects you with websites that satisfy your query. Thompson suggests that successful aggregators have three main characteristics: They own the relationship with the user, there is zero (or very low) marginal cost to serve new users, and the cost to acquire users goes down as the result of positive feedback. Other examples of aggregators include Netflix, Airbnb, and Amazon.com.
- *Platform companies.* Platform companies facilitate the relationship between third-party suppliers and end users. One example is Shopify, which operates an e-commerce platform for stores and provides retail point-of-sale systems. Shopify does not deal directly with the customers of the merchants on its platform. Rather, it provides those merchants with the tools they need to be effective in the market. These businesses create an ecosystem and take a small amount of the value created. Other examples of platforms include Stripe, Microsoft's Windows ecosystem, and Amazon Web Services.

Aggregators enjoy economies of scale that create a formidable barrier to entry. Platforms become integral to ecosystems such that they create substantial switching costs for users. That many of these companies invest primarily in intangible assets does not obviate the importance of industry drivers and specific sources of competitive advantage.

In a digital world, customers are increasingly turning to subscriptions to address needs and desires. We used to stuff physical photos in a shoebox but now have a subscription to store them digitally on iCloud Photos. Trips to the movie theater have been partially replaced by a remote control and a Netflix subscription. Companies used to buy prepackaged software but now subscribe to software as a service (SaaS).

Daniel McCarthy and Peter Fader, professors of marketing, have developed what they call "customer-based corporate valuation," or CBCV.[20] This approach values a company from the bottom up by analyzing the economics of customer relationships. The value of a customer is the difference between the present value of the cash flows the customer generates during his or her tenure and the cost to acquire the customer. Cash flows are revenues minus all associated costs. Customer retention is commonly expressed as churn, or the percentage of customers that stop using a company's product or service during a certain period.

The concept of customer lifetime value has been around for decades. CBCV's main contribution is the ability to accurately forecast sales growth. This is extremely useful as sales growth is commonly the most important value driver. To do a proper CBCV analysis, you need a customer acquisition model to understand how fast new customers are added, a customer retention model to understand how long they will remain active buyers, a purchase model to understand how often they will buy, and a model to understand how much they will purchase when they do transact.[21] Most companies do not disclose information in this much detail, but in many cases it is possible to make educated estimates.

McCarthy and Fader use these models to generate revenue forecasts and then subtract relevant costs to define free cash flow. Their valuation model is based on traditional discounted cash flow. We include this discussion under information economics because it is common for customer acquisition costs to show up on the income statement as expenses. Examples of these costs include marketing and free trials.

While you can use CBCV to estimate the value of a company, we believe it is even more powerful as a tool for expectations investing. A company's stock price allows you to determine what key customer metrics you need to believe to justify the prevailing price. In turn, the economics of customer businesses rely in large part on the industry in which the company competes and its strategic position.

Expectations investing is not just about prospective changes in operating value drivers. It helps investors make informed judgments about where to find potentially profitable opportunities by integrating the expectations infrastructure with competitive strategy analysis.

Essential Ideas

- The surest path to anticipating revisions in expectations is to foresee shifts in a company's competitive dynamics.
- Management and investors have different performance hurdles. Management tries to achieve returns above the cost of capital. Investors try to anticipate changes in market expectations correctly.
- Historical performance and the lay of the land provide insight into potential value driver variability by showing which operating value drivers have been most variable in the past and how stable the industry appears to be. This

type of analysis provides a reality check on the ranges of expectations.

- The five forces model helps illuminate the drivers of industry profitability, and the disruptive innovation model reveals potential vulnerability and opportunity.
- A firm creates value when the willingness to pay of its customers exceeds the firm's opportunity cost. Companies can gain an advantage by having above-average willingness to pay (differentiation), below-average cost (cost leadership), or a combination. Value chain analysis helps pinpoint the sources of advantage.
- The laws of economics have not changed, but it is important to recognize that physical and knowledge businesses have different characteristics.

PART II

Implementing the Process

5

How to Estimate Price-Implied Expectations

AN INVESTOR MUST correctly anticipate revisions in the stock market's expectations to earn superior investment returns. But you need to clearly understand where expectations stand today before you can consider the likelihood and magnitude of expectations revisions.

Ask an average group of investors if they are interested in understanding market expectations, and you'll hear a resounding yes. But if you ask them how they go about reading the market, they'll probably fall back on a slew of contemporaneous, statistical benchmarks such as short-term earnings and price-earnings multiples. Though ubiquitous, these investment shorthands simply don't paint an economically sound picture of today's expectations because they aren't reliably linked to shareholder value.

You must think in the market's terms to accurately read the expectations wrapped in stock prices. The long-term discounted cash flow model best captures the stock market's pricing mechanism. Yet investors justifiably think that forecasting distant cash flows is extraordinarily hazardous. Credible long-term forecasts are difficult to make and often reveal only the underlying biases of the investor making the forecast. As Warren Buffett says, "Forecasts usually tell us more of the forecaster than of the future."[1] Where, then, do you turn?

The ideal solution allows you to use the discounted cash flow model without the burden of cash flow forecasts. This is precisely what expectations investing does. Instead of forecasting cash flows, expectations investing starts with the current stock price and uses the discounted cash flow model to "read" what the market implies about a company's future performance. This estimate of price-implied expectations (PIE) launches the expectations investing process (figure 5.1).

Think about it this way: It's hard for an individual to forecast an uncertain future better than the collective wisdom of the market can. So why not get the PIE directly from the source?

Many investors and executives view stock prices with some misgiving, perceiving that prices don't always accurately convey value. But expectations investors take a different view. For them, stock price is the best and least exploited information source available. Stock price, the dollar level at which buyers and sellers are willing to transact, is the clearest and most reliable indicator of the market's expectations at any given time. You just need to know how to read the market today and anticipate what the expectations are likely to be tomorrow.

One final thought before we explain how to read expectations. We have conducted expectations analysis on many stocks in our roles as teachers, security analysts, and consultants. The results typically surprise investors and corporate executives.

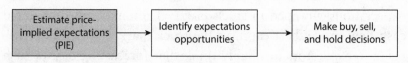

FIGURE 5.1 Expectations investing process.

Investors who assume that the market focuses on the short term are amazed to find that it actually takes a long-term view. Corporate executives, who instinctively believe that the market undervalues their company's stock, are often startled to find that the market's expectations are more ambitious than their own. So be prepared to be surprised the first few times you read PIE.

Reading Expectations

In chapter 2, we showed that a combination of free cash flows, the cost of capital, and a forecast period determines value in a discounted cash flow model. We also noted that expectations investing uses the same computational tools but reverses the process by starting with the stock price and then estimating the expectations for cash flow, the cost of capital, and the forecast horizon that justify the stock price.

Here are some operational guidelines on how to read expectations. Although you should find these tips useful, be aware that reading expectations is as much an art as it is a science. The ability to read expectations improves with experience and industry knowledge.

Finally, you should go into this step of the expectations investing process without any preconceived notions. Try to be agnostic about the outcomes for now. Your goal at this point is to read the mind of the market. You'll have the opportunity to assess the reasonableness of those expectations in another step.

Cash Flows

You can consult a number of sources to establish the market's consensus forecast for sales growth rate, operating profit margin, and incremental investment rate. These include *Value Line Investment Survey, Morningstar, FactSet, Bloomberg, S&P Capital IQ,*

Refinitiv, Wall Street reports, and information that management provides to investors. To assess the reasonableness of the consensus forecast for value drivers, evaluate the industry environment in light of competitive circumstances. Finally, review historical value driver performance and note any meaningful differences between past and expected performance.

Cost of Capital

Use the approach outlined in chapter 2, "How the Market Values Stocks," to estimate a company's weighted average cost of capital. Here is some additional guidance:[2]

- *Bloomberg* and *FactSet* are among the several services that estimate the cost of capital.
- Betas are available from multiple sources, including *Bloomberg*, *Value Line*, *S&P Capital IQ*, and *Yahoo Finance*.
- Forward-looking market risk premium estimates are available from Aswath Damodaran, a professor of finance, as well as various brokerage and advisory firms such as Duff & Phelps.

Nonoperating Assets and Debt

You generally do not have to estimate nonoperating assets or corporate liabilities such as interest-bearing debt or underfunded pension funds, because they appear on the balance sheet.

Common nonoperating assets include excess cash and marketable securities, nonconsolidated subsidiaries and investments in affiliated companies, overfunded pension plans, and tax loss carryforwards. Make sure to consider the difference between the value recorded on the balance sheet and market value, as well as tax consequences, when estimating the value of nonoperating assets and liabilities.

Market-Implied Forecast Period

The final value determinant is the number of years of free cash flows required to justify the stock price. We call this horizon the market-implied forecast period. (It's also called "value growth duration" and "competitive advantage period" and is consistent with the idea of "fade rate.")[3]

Practically, the market-implied forecast period measures how long the market expects a company to generate returns on its incremental investments that exceed its cost of capital. The model assumes that the additional investments a company makes after the market-implied forecast period will earn the cost of capital, and consequently add no further value. The market-implied forecast period for U.S. stocks clusters between five and fifteen years, but it can be in a range from zero to as long as thirty years for companies with strong competitive positions.[4]

You can solve for the market-implied forecast period once you've determined the market's expectations for future free cash flows and the cost of capital. You do that by lengthening the forecast horizon in the discounted cash flow model as many years as it takes to arrive at today's stock price. For example, if you must extend your discounted free cash flows (plus continuing value) twelve years to reach a company's current stock price, the market-implied forecast period is twelve years.

Domino's Pizza Case Study

Let's make this concept more concrete by doing the analysis on the stock of Domino's Pizza, a multinational pizza restaurant chain.

When we analyzed the stock in August 2020, Domino's had 39.3 million shares outstanding and traded at around $418, for a market capitalization of about $16 billion.

Cash Flows

To estimate the expectations that the $418 price implied, we reviewed *Morningstar*, *Value Line*, and analyst forecasts. We reached the following consensus forecast:

Sales growth rate	7.0%
Operating profit margin	17.5%
Cash tax rate	16.5%
Incremental fixed-capital rate	10.0%
Incremental working-capital rate	15.0%

The sales growth rate, operating profit margin, and cash tax rate determine net operating profit after taxes (NOPAT). Incremental fixed-capital and working-capital rates tell us that for every incremental dollar of sales, Domino's will invest $0.10 in fixed capital, or capital expenditures minus depreciation, and $0.15 in working capital. This is our best estimate of the market's view of Domino's expected operating value driver performance.

Cost of Capital

At the time of the analysis, the yield on the risk-free U.S. ten-year Treasury note was 0.65 percent, the market risk premium estimate was 5.1 percent, and beta was 1.0. To estimate the beta, we started with the unlevered beta for the industry and levered it to reflect Domino's capital structure. Although the beta calculated using the stock price was lower than 1.0, the industry figure better represented the risk in our judgment. Accordingly, Domino's cost of equity was 5.75 percent [0.65% + (1.0 × 5.1%) = 5.75%].

Domino's pretax cost of debt was 4.55 percent, making its after-tax cost of debt 3.8 percent [4.55% × (1 – 16.5%) = 3.80%]. Domino's debt-to-total capital ratio is about 20 percent. So its weighted average cost of capital was 5.35 percent [(0.80 × 5.75%) + (0.20 × 3.80%) = 5.35%].

Nonoperating Assets and Debt

At the end of 2019, Domino's had nonoperating assets consisting of excess cash and marketable securities of about $390 million, or approximately $10.00 per share. Domino's liabilities, almost exclusively debt, totaled roughly $4.1 billion, or $105 per share.

Market-Implied Forecast Period

Here is how we calculate Domino's market-implied forecast period of eight years. Starting in year 2020, we calculate Domino's shareholder value per share at the end of each year (table 5.1). Note that we use the perpetuity-with-inflation method for the continuing value because we believe that Domino's net operating profit after taxes (NOPAT) and investments will increase in line with inflation following the market-implied forecast period. We then extend the forecast period as far as necessary to reach the current stock price.

We estimate Domino's value at the end of 2020 to be $285 per share, and it increases each year until it reaches its $418 stock price at the end of 2027, the eighth year. The market-implied forecast period is therefore eight years.

Table 5.1
Calculation of market-implied forecast period for Domino's Pizza (in millions)

	2019	2020	2021	2022	2023	2024	2025	2026	2027
Sales	$3,618.8	$3,872.1	$4,143.1	$4,433.1	$4,743.5	$5,075.5	$5,430.8	$5,811.0	$6,217.7
Operating profit	629.4	677.6	725.0	775.8	830.1	888.2	950.4	1,016.9	1,088.1
Less: Cash taxes on operating profit	105.2	111.8	119.6	128.0	137.0	146.6	156.8	167.8	179.5
Net operating profit after taxes (NOPAT)	524.2	565.8	605.4	647.8	693.1	741.7	793.6	849.1	908.6
Incremental working-capital investment		25.3	27.1	29.0	31.0	33.2	35.5	38.0	40.7
Incremental fixed-capital investment		38.0	40.7	43.5	46.5	49.8	53.3	57.0	61.0
Investment		63.3	67.8	72.5	77.6	83.0	88.8	95.0	101.7
Free cash flow		502.5	537.7	575.3	615.6	658.6	704.8	754.1	806.9
Present value of free cash flow		476.9	484.4	491.9	499.6	507.4	515.3	523.3	531.5
Cumulative present value of free cash flow		476.9	961.3	1,453.2	1,952.8	2,460.2	2,975.5	3,498.8	4,030.3
Present value of continuing value		14,523.2	14,749.7	14,979.7	15,213.3	15,450.6	15,691.5	15,936.2	16,184.8
Corporate value		15,000.1	15,711.0	16,432.9	17,166.1	17,910.8	18,667.0	19,435.1	20,215.1
Add: Nonoperating assets		391.9	391.9	391.9	391.9	391.9	391.9	391.9	391.9
Less: Debt and other liabilities		4,170.0	4,170.0	4,170.0	4,170.0	4,170.0	4,170.0	4,170.0	4,170.0
Shareholder value		11,222.0	11,932.9	12,654.8	13,388.0	14,132.7	14,888.9	15,656.9	16,437.0
Shareholder value per share		$285.18	$303.25	$321.60	$340.23	$359.15	$378.37	$397.89	$417.71

Why Revisit Expectations?

Chapter 12 is dedicated to the sources of opportunities for expectations revisions. But you should be prepared to revisit PIE either when a stock price changes significantly or when a company discloses important new information. Frequently, both happen at the same time.

For example, companies that experience relatively large stock-price responses to earnings surprises are logical candidates for a fresh look at expectations. Earnings surprises, favorable and unfavorable, sometimes lead to a market overreaction.

Consider the November 2019 announcement by Plantronics, a communications equipment manufacturer. Plantronics missed sales and earnings estimates, reduced guidance, and stated that it would reduce inventory of its products in its sales channel. Notwithstanding that the company suggested its revenue shortfall was "driven by factors that are transitory" and reiterated its long-term prospects, the market's response was a swift and brutal 37 percent stock-price decline.[5] If a company's statement signals lower expectations for long-term revenue and earnings, then the steep decline is warranted. On the other hand, if the interruption in growth is truly temporary, a lower stock price may represent a buying opportunity.

Examples of important new information include merger and acquisition deals, significant share buyback programs, and meaningful changes in executive incentive compensation. We address the signaling implications of mergers and acquisitions in chapter 10 and of buyback programs in chapter 11.

Essential Ideas

- To read expectations properly, you must think in the market's terms. Expectations investing allows you to tap the benefits of the discounted cash flow model without requiring you to forecast long-term cash flows.

- You need to clearly understand where expectations stand today before you can consider the likelihood and magnitude of expectations revisions.
- You can estimate PIE by using publicly available information sources.
- You should consider revisiting an expectations analysis when stock prices change significantly or when a company discloses important new information.

6

Identifying Expectations Opportunities

WE NOW TURN to the second step of the expectations investing process, identifying expectations opportunities (figure 6.1). Some revisions in expectations are inevitably more important than others. Focusing on what matters allows you to allocate your time more efficiently and to increase your odds of finding high potential payoffs.

The first thing you want to do is isolate the value trigger that is likely to have the greatest impact on shareholder value. We call this the turbo trigger. Just as a turbo charger on a car substantially increases its power, the turbo trigger gives you the ability to figure out what matters most. The goal is to improve the chance of finding a meaningful difference between the current price-implied expectations (PIE) and future revisions.

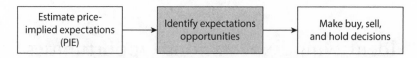

FIGURE 6.1 Expectations investing process.

Searching for Expectations Opportunities

The foundation for identifying expectations opportunities includes two data sets and two tools (figure 6.2). The data sets are historical performance and PIE, the market's expectations for a company's future performance. Past performance serves as a reality check on the reasonableness of PIE and your assessment of likely revisions.

The tools are the expectations infrastructure (chapter 3) and competitive strategy analysis (chapter 4). The expectations infrastructure allows for systematic analysis of the underlying sources of shareholder value. Competitive strategy analysis allows you to

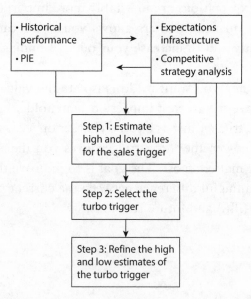

FIGURE 6.2 Identifying expectations opportunities.

assess industry attractiveness and a company's chosen strategies. Together these tools yield indispensable insights into potential revisions of market expectations.

Assessing the Triggers

Anticipating expectations opportunities has a few steps that will allow you to identify the turbo trigger and to refine your estimates of its impact on shareholder value.

Step 1: Estimate High and Low Values for the Sales Trigger and Calculate the Shareholder Values That Result

We begin with the sales trigger because revisions in sales are likely to produce the most significant changes in shareholder value. Starting with sales also allows you to quickly determine whether you should spend time on the other two value triggers, operating costs and investments. This substantially reduces your analytical effort because you focus on what matters.

To estimate the impact of the sales trigger on shareholder value, you first need to estimate a range of sales growth rates, including high and low scenarios. Use the benchmark data (historical performance and PIE) and analytical tools (the expectations infrastructure and competitive strategy analysis) to create these forecasts.

The essential exercise is to carefully consider the connections between the sales growth rates and the four value factors: volume, price and mix, operating leverage, and economies of scale. This will allow you to assess how various sales growth rates affect the operating profit margin and, accordingly, the corresponding shareholder values. Study the results. The range depicts the change in stock price from potential sales growth variability.

For some companies, especially those with substantial operating leverage, the value factors driven by sales will have a large positive or negative impact on operating profit margins. In other cases, value factors mutually offset one another. For example, market-leading companies such as Walmart and Costco pass on the benefits of economies of scale and cost efficiencies to their consumers through lower prices. And for yet other firms, the result of sales changes does not affect operating profit margin enough to justify detailed analysis.

This step also defines how great the shareholder value variability must be for one of the other two triggers, costs or investments, to qualify as the turbo trigger.

Step 2: Select the Turbo Trigger

You can figure out whether costs or investments qualify as the turbo trigger by determining how far they must vary from their PIE estimates to have a greater impact on shareholder value than does the sales trigger.

Assume that you estimate the PIE for a stock that currently trades at $20. The high and low estimates of the sales growth rate, filtered through the expectations infrastructure, yield values of $30 and $10, respectively. Use the expectations infrastructure to calculate the high and low operating profit margins, solely as the result of cost efficiencies, required to create a comparable impact on shareholder value. Look at the result and consider the likelihood that the margin will be that variable.

For example, suppose the $20 stock price implies an operating profit margin of 10 percent, that the high sales growth rate estimate supports a $30 stock price and a 17 percent margin, and that the low sales growth rate estimate suggests a $10 stock price and a 3 percent margin. You can then assess if potential cost savings are sufficient to qualify as the turbo trigger. You can apply the same procedure to test the changes in the incremental investment rate for the investments trigger.

In the case that shareholder value is sufficiently sensitive to either cost or investment variability to qualify as the turbo trigger, you should revisit that trigger, estimate high and low ranges for

WHAT ABOUT THE COST OF CAPITAL AND THE MARKET-IMPLIED FORECAST PERIOD?

The search for expectations opportunities should primarily focus on the value triggers and the value driver projections they spawn, not the cost of capital or the market-implied forecast period. Here's why.

Let's start with the cost of capital. Changes in interest rates influence stock prices because they affect discount rates. Often, changes in interest rates, rather than revisions in performance expectations, explain stock-price movements. However, relying on interest rate forecasts for the purpose of individual stock selection is a losing game. Shifts in interest rates affect all stocks, albeit to different degrees. Rebalance your mix of stocks, bonds, and cash if you feel strongly about the direction of interest rates.

In our experience, the forecast periods of companies within the same industry are usually narrowly clustered. If a company's market-implied forecast period is substantially longer or shorter than that of its industry peers, then you should carefully recheck the PIE value drivers to be certain that you have accurately reflected the consensus. Assuming that the company's competitive profile is close to the industry average, a relatively short market-implied forecast period may signal a buying opportunity and a long period may signal a selling opportunity.

A constant market-implied forecast period is tantamount to a continual change in expectations. For example, assume that a company's forecast period is four years today and that it remains unchanged a year from now. If there truly were no change in expectations, the market-implied forecast period a year from now would be three years rather than four. In this case, an investor who purchased shares priced with four years of value creation expectations receives a bonus of an additional year. This positive shift in expectations would create an extra return, assuming that there are no offsetting expectations changes in the company's operating value drivers.

the affected value drivers (either operating profit margin or incremental investment rate), and calculate the resulting high and low shareholder values.

Step 3: Refine the High and Low Estimates of the Turbo Trigger and Calculate the Shareholder Values That Result

You should refine your initial estimates of turbo trigger variability before you decide to buy, sell, or hold. Specifically, drill down one more level to the leading indicators of value. Leading indicators are measurable, current accomplishments that significantly affect the turbo trigger and hence shareholder value. Examples include customer retention rates, time to market for new products, number of on-time new-store openings, quality improvements, and average cycle time from order date to shipping date. Two or three key leading indicators typically account for a substantial percentage of the variability in the turbo trigger.

Pitfalls to Avoid

We all occasionally fall into psychological traps that keep us from achieving higher investment returns. These traps materialize when we use rules of thumb, or heuristics, to reduce the information demands of effective decision making. While heuristics simplify analysis, they can also lead to biases that undermine the quality of our decisions. Intuition often suggests a course of action that more deliberate analysis proves to be suboptimal. Be sure to avoid two common biases, overconfidence and confirmation, when you establish the range of potential expectations revisions. Let's look at these pitfalls more closely.

Researchers find that people consistently overrate their abilities, knowledge, and skill. This is especially relevant in areas outside their expertise. This overconfidence takes a few forms. One is overestimation, which means you think you are better at something than you really are. Another is overplacement, the sense that you are better than others at certain tasks. The form that is important for us is overprecision, which means that you are surer about your knowledge than you should be.[1] For example, when security analysts responded to requests for information that they were unlikely to know (e.g., the total land area of Africa in square miles or kilometers), they chose ranges wide enough to accommodate the correct answer only 64 percent of the time. Money managers were even less successful, at 50 percent.[2]

Remember the concept of overprecision when you estimate the high and low scenarios for sales growth as part of the initial step in the search for expectations opportunities. A frequent error is to consider a range of outcomes that is insufficiently wide. For example, if your estimated range is too narrow, you may misidentify the turbo trigger as costs or investments when, in fact, you should select sales. You can get misleading signals when you estimate inappropriate ranges.

How do you avoid overprecision? There are several simple and practical ways:

- Compare the range to past results for the company, its peers, and a broader population of firms.
- Seek feedback from others.
- Keep track of past analyses and learn from your mistakes.

The second pitfall is confirmation bias, which occurs when we seek information that confirms our beliefs and dismiss, disregard, or discount information that runs against our view. This bias can cause errors in two parts of the expectations investing process. One is when you are reading price-implied expectations. The goal is to suspend your views and to be as impartial as possible. Only after you understand the market's view should you introduce your own analysis.

Another is when you are updating your view based on the arrival of new information. We all want to be right when we make a decision and are therefore reticent to acknowledge information that suggests we are wrong. Experiments reveal that investors are more likely to read articles that support their view than those that run counter to it.[3] Bright people are particularly vulnerable because they are exceptionally good at justifying their beliefs.

How do you avoid confirmation bias? You can take some of the following precautions:

- Leave aside your beliefs as you do a PIE analysis.
- View the decision from various points of view.
- Document your views and be disciplined about updating them when new information justifies doing so.

Domino's Pizza Case Study

We will now reinforce the analytical terrain we just covered by continuing the case study of Domino's Pizza. We didn't delve into the strategy and operations for Domino's in the last chapter because our goal was to estimate PIE. We now need to enlist the full set of tools to create a more complete picture of the company.

Domino's Pizza is the largest pizza company in the world based on retail sales. As of the end of 2019, the company had more than 17,000 locations in over 90 markets around the world and retail sales of more than $14 billion. About 35 percent of the stores are in the United States, and the rest are international. Nearly all its stores are owned and operated by independent franchisees. The few hundred stores that Domino's operates allow it to test new technology, the efficacy of promotions, and operational improvements.

The primary way that Domino's makes money is by charging its franchisees royalties and fees based on their revenues. In the United States, the company deals directly with its franchisees. In international markets, the company has master franchisees, which have geographical rights to the brand. This tells us that the financial health of the franchisees is critical to the company's success.

Domino's supply chain operations, which provide food and other items to stores in the United States and selected international markets, are its largest segment. This business allows the franchisees to have inputs of consistent quality, to leverage technology through ordering and inventory management, and to benefit from economies of scale. The supply chain business has profit-sharing arrangements with those franchisees that rely on the service exclusively. This provides the franchisees with an important source of profits and aligns the interests of the franchisees with those of the parent company.

Domino's participates primarily in the delivery and carryout segments of the pizza industry. In the United States, industry sales were roughly $38 billion in 2019, half of which was carryout, 30 percent delivery, and 20 percent dine-in. Domino's has 16 percent share of the carryout segment and 35 percent share of the delivery segment.[4]

Domino's is a leader in the restaurant industry in its use of technology and data, which is important because more than one-half of its global retail sales came from digital channels such as computers, mobile phones, and smartwatches. The company learns a great deal about end users through these orders, allowing it to anticipate demand, evaluate the payoff from new products and promotions, and manage labor and inventory costs. Domino's has more than 25 million active users in its loyalty program and 85 million customers in its database.

Competitive Analysis

The goal of strategy analysis is to anticipate potential revisions in expectations. Following with the framework for assessing strategy that we outlined in chapter 4, we get the lay of the land for Domino's to understand the competitive landscape, do an industry analysis to assess market characteristics, and finish with a focus on the firm's specific advantages.

Figure 6.3 shows an industry map for the pizza industry. A few points are noteworthy. First, Domino's competes with a number of other large national and international pizza chains, but mom-and-pop stores are about 40 percent of the market. Beyond pizza, there are other formidable competitors in the quick-serve restaurant industry, including companies such as McDonald's, Chick-fil-A, and Yum! Brands (which owns Pizza Hut, KFC, and Taco Bell). Second, franchisees are important to the industry, so understanding their financial health is crucial. And finally, the map shows how customers interact with the pizza companies. Of note, Domino's does not compete in the dine-in segment of the market. Digital channels allow the company to gather substantial customer information that enables it to ground its decisions in data.

We will not do a full value pool analysis, but it is clear that the profitability of franchisees is core to this analysis. Said simply,

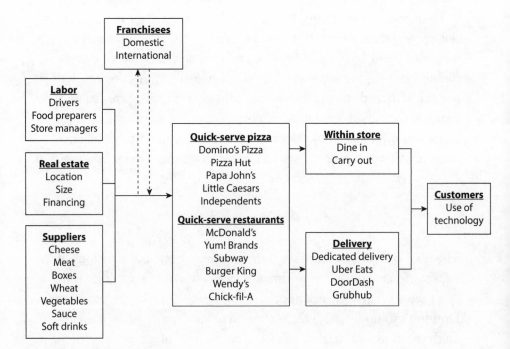

FIGURE 6.3 Industry map.

since Domino's revenues are a direct function of the sales of its franchisees, it wants happy and healthy franchisees that are keen to grow. In fact, when compared to Pizza Hut and Papa John's, its largest competitors in the United States, Domino's has among the lowest costs of building and opening a new restaurant and among the highest profits per store. Domino's stores have cash-on-cash returns, defined as annual pretax cash flow divided by the total amount of cash invested, in excess of 40 percent, versus an average in the quick-serve restaurant industry of 15 to 20 percent.[5]

In 2012, the company adopted a strategy of "fortressing": adding more stores to a geographic market to increase density. This strategy improves customer service, allows delivery drivers to stay busier and therefore earn more, and expands carryout sales. Average U.S. franchisee store profits, measured as earnings before interest, taxes, depreciation, and amortization, doubled from 2011 to 2019.

Franchisee profitability is also a leading indicator of value. The sales growth rate of Domino's is hitched to the growth of its franchisees.

The market share test, table 6.1, reveals a couple of noteworthy points. Domino's has enjoyed strong market share gains in recent years, even as some other large chains have lost ground. This is against the backdrop of a category that has grown just under 2 percent over the past five years. Independents also lost some share, which is consistent with a secular trend. The overall change in market share is relatively low when compared to other industries, suggesting relative stability.

We now turn to industry analysis. We focus on the five forces that affect expectations because we do not deem Domino's to be at great risk of being disrupted:

- *Substitution threat.* We can think of substitution threats, which are significant, in two ways. The first is alternative food choices. Pizza competes with lots of other offerings, and customers can readily substitute one selection for another. The steady growth of the pizza category suggests

Table 6.1
Market share test

Pizza restaurants (US by sales)	2014 (%)	2019 (%)	Five-year absolute change (%)
Domino's	9.9	14.2	4.4
Pizza Hut	14.8	11.9	2.9
Little Caesars	7.9	7.9	0.1
Papa John's	6.4	5.9	0.5
Other chains	20.1	20.1	0.1
Independents	40.9	40.0	0.9
Total	100	100	
Average absolute change			1.5

Source: Technomic and CHD Expert.

that consumers continue to find value and enjoyment in the category. The other threat is the mode of delivery. In recent years, food delivery aggregators such as DoorDash and Uber Eats have emerged as intermediaries between restaurants and consumers. In the early years, these businesses have been backed by substantial capital, leading to aggressive promotion and discounting in the market. The restaurant industry value chain is likely to reorganize to serve these aggregators, which will offer consumers ample opportunity to switch between food choices at a low cost.

- *Buyer power.* Domino's has positioned itself in the value segment of the market. This is supported by its efficient supply chain system. By keeping prices and costs low, Domino's has not been challenged by this force. This conclusion is further supported by healthy franchisee profits.
- *Supplier power.* This force is also not a major source of concern for Domino's. The company's largest commodity costs are cheese, meat, boxes, wheat, vegetables, and

sauce. Domino's has long-term contracts to acquire these inputs from suppliers, and the company believes that it could turn to third-party suppliers without imposing a meaningful adverse impact on the business. Domino's scale and density also allow it to provide competitive pay for food preparers and drivers. Labor and food costs are 50 to 60 percent of sales at the stores owned by Domino's.

- *Barriers to entry.* On the surface, barriers to entry do not appear particularly high in the pizza business because capital commitments are relatively modest and the product itself is simple. But the fact that independent restaurants have lost modest share to chains suggests that it is tough to crack the business profitably. Large incumbents have advantages that include economies of scale in activities such as procurement and advertising, brands that reduce search costs, and substantial data on consumer taste and behavior. The handful of new chains that have launched in recent decades remain a relatively small part of the overall market.

- *Rivalry among competitors.* There is plenty of competition in the pizza industry, but Domino's is the largest in the world based on retail sales, and its store-level returns are among the most attractive. Price competition is a classic signal of rivalry. It is very difficult for competitors to undercut Domino's prices because Domino's is already positioned in the value segment and has low costs. Fortressing also provides for local economies of scale that make it difficult for rivals to compete effectively against Domino's.

Industry structure determines profitability, and the U.S. restaurant industry creates value overall. While some franchise owners in other chains and smaller operations struggle to add value, the structure is sufficiently healthy to allow Domino's to achieve attractive profitability at the store level. This means that the parent company creates substantial value.

FIGURE 6.4 The value chain. From Joan Magretta, *Understanding Michael Porter: The Essential Guide to Competition and Strategy* (Boston, MA: Harvard Business Review Press, 2012), 76. Used by permission.

A firm creates value when it receives more for its goods or services than it costs to produce them, including the opportunity cost of capital. We just saw that the industry is solidly profitable and that Domino's has an attractive position within the industry. We now turn to value chain analysis to understand what distinguishes Domino's from its competitors and to assess whether these advantages may be subject to revisions in expectations (figure 6.4).

The first step in value chain analysis is to understand the industry. Restaurants are a reasonably straightforward business. The store receives supplies, prepares food and drink, and serves it to customers. These basic activities are common among all restaurants.

Domino's supply chain business allows most of its stores in North America to receive inputs that are of consistent quality and at competitive prices as the result of scale. The supply chain business is not meant to be a profit center but rather operates to facilitate attractive franchisee economics. Other chains also have dedicated supply companies, but smaller operators generally rely on food distribution businesses that are not as aligned with the restaurants or suited to the specifics of each store's menu.

Strategy boils down to trade-offs, and perhaps Domino's most important decision is not to provide meaningful dine-in options. This choice allows for the stores to be smaller and cheaper. It also allows for operational simplicity and efficiency in preparing food, and for more efficient use of labor.

At the same time, Domino's is organized to be highly efficient in delivery and carryout. This efficiency is further enhanced by local economies of scale via high store density. The company's orders per market per hour are well above the industry average, which allows for a better consumer experience via faster delivery and better store profitability.

Technology also differentiates Domino's from its peers. It has long been a leader in digital systems, including its PULSE system for point of sales that helps franchisees be more efficient and provides valuable information to the company's management.

Competitive strategy analysis suggests that Domino's competes in a relatively stable industry that creates modest value in the aggregate. The company has added substantial value through strategic decisions to focus on delivery and carryout versus dining in and to ensure that franchisee economics are attractive via the application of technology and a fortressing approach. The company also takes advantage of economies of scale in procurement, technology, and advertising.

Historical Analysis

An analysis of historical financial results (table 6.2) offers the following clues about future performance variability:

Table 6.2
Domino's Pizza historical operating value drivers

	2015	2016	2017	2018	2019	Five-year average
Sales growth rate (%)	11.2	11.6	12.8	23.1	5.4	12.7
Operating profit margin (%)	18.3	18.4	18.7	16.7	17.4	17.7
Incremental fixed-capital investment rate (%)	13.9	8.0	14.5	10.3	13.8	13.7
Incremental working-capital investment rate (%)	–9.0	–1.3	10.6	7.5	–3.1	3.2

Source: Domino's Pizza, Inc.
Note: Five-year average sales growth is geometric.

- *Sales growth* advanced at a healthy double-digit clip in the last five years, although about 2.5 percentage points of the increase was the result of an accounting change. The supply chain business was the largest contributor to the increase in dollar sales, and that business mirrors the growth in the number of stores owned and franchised in North America. Overall, the number of U.S. franchise stores grew 4.3 percent per year and average same-store sales increased 8.0 percent. International operations grew the store count by 10.7 percent annually and had same-store sales growth of 4.6 percent. International sales rose at a rate consistent with the overall company, reflecting the negative impact of currency exchange on sales growth.

- *Operating profit margin* was in a consistent range from a low of 16.7 percent in 2018 to a high of 18.7 percent in 2017. Over a longer period, operating profit margins have expanded as the company has enjoyed the benefit of operating leverage. Note that the company runs the supply chain business to have low gross margins, generally close to 11 percent. The company has managed general and administrative expenses well, and advertising expense is consistently more than 10 percent of revenues.

- *Investments.* Domino's business does not require substantial capital. The incremental fixed-capital investment rate averaged under 15 percent in recent years, with the spending largely dedicated to technology for point-of-sales systems, expansion of supply chain operations, and new and upgraded company-owned stores. Working-capital needs are not material. Note that much of the investment burden falls on the franchisees, which is why ensuring their health is central to the success of Domino's.

Identifying Expectations Opportunities for Domino's

The competitive and historical analyses indicate that sales growth is the most likely turbo trigger. But let's go to the numbers to confirm this conclusion.

Below are the consensus forecasts for Domino's price-implied expectations that we introduced in chapter 5. The numbers reflect an August 2020 stock price of $418 and consensus forecasts from *Value Line* and analyst reports. The competitive analysis and historical overview provide the background for the three steps for identifying expectations opportunities.

Sales growth rate	7.0%
Operating profit margin	17.5%
Cash tax rate	16.5%
Incremental fixed-capital rate	10.0%
Incremental working-capital rate	15.0%

Step 1: Estimate High and Low Values for the Sales Trigger and Calculate the Shareholder Values That Result

Our analysis and reviews of the work of leading analysts point to a sales growth range of 3 to 11 percent over the eight-year forecast period. In practice, we encourage multiple scenarios. We show the low, high, and consensus in order to simplify the exposition. Here's the rationale for what we selected:

- *Low.* Assumes that store growth and same-store sales in the United States and internationally are well below historical standards and company guidance. Company-owned stores also achieve sales increases less than in the past, and the supply chain business grows in line with domestic sales. In this scenario, Domino's falls short of achieving the opportunity it projects.

- *High*. Reflects low double-digit sales growth in the United States and internationally, consistent with a rapid rate of store openings and same-store sales gains. The supply chain top line advance is similar to that of the U.S. business, and company-owned stores have high-single-digit top line growth.

Domino's Pizza is unlike many other businesses in that its value-creating revenues come mostly from royalties and fees collected from franchisees. As a result, the company's primary goal is to foster franchise health through the application of technology, effective advertising, and low-cost supplies.

The expectations infrastructure helps us translate the turbo trigger, sales growth, into the operating value drivers. The first two value factors are volume and price and mix. Domino's is distinct relative to the quick-serve pizza category in that it has driven sales increases primarily through a higher number of orders, which is a proxy for volume, and has seen limited ticket growth, which reflects price and mix. The rest of the quick-serve pizza industry has advanced solely through ticket growth in recent years.

Domino's benefits from both operating leverage and economies of scale, but the impact on operating profit margins is ultimately muted. One example of operating leverage is the deployment of technology, where the up-front costs can be expensive but are relatively cheap when distributed over a large number of locations. Economies of scale exist in the supply chain operations and allow franchisees to maintain low costs, which they can pass on to consumers.

An analysis of the historical relationship between sales changes and operating profit shows the benefits of operating leverage and economies of scale. That said, Domino's prefers to pass on savings rather than earn more at the parent level because it believes that making sure franchisees thrive is key to maximizing long-term value.

Reflecting these considerations, an assumption of a high sales growth rate leads to a 100-basis-point improvement in operating profit margin, and a low case shows a 100-basis-point decline.

We are now ready to determine the impact of a change in the sales growth rate on shareholder value. Here are the numbers:

Sales growth rate			Estimated value		Change in value	
PIE	Low	High	Low	High	Low	High
7%	3%	11%	$290	$586	−30.6%	40.2%

These data tell us that if we were to lower expectations for Domino's sales growth rate from 7 percent to 3 percent, the stock would retreat by 30 percent, from roughly $418 to $290 per share. Alternatively, an upward shift in anticipated sales growth from 7 percent to 11 percent would spark a 40 percent rise to $586 per share.

Step 2: Select the Turbo Trigger

What would it take for the costs and investments triggers to change value more than sales does? Cost efficiencies, or ineffi-ciencies, would have to add or subtract more than 4 percentage points, or 400 basis points, to the PIE operating profit margin of 17.5 percent in order to be as material as sales growth. Given Domino's cost structure, that magnitude of expectations revision seems highly unlikely. We can conclude that operating costs will not be as important as sales.

Changes in the incremental fixed-capital rate and incremental working-capital rate would need to undergo extreme revisions to have an impact comparable to that of sales. Domino's business model, competitive landscape, and historical results all suggest that such an outcome is improbable. We can safely conclude that investment is a less significant trigger than sales. The analysis con-firms that sales is the turbo trigger for Domino's.

Step 3: Refine the High and Low Estimates of the Turbo Trigger and Calculate the Shareholder Values That Result

WHAT'S IN A TARGET PRICE?

Our . . . $420 price target is based on ~30× new C[alendar] [20]22 EPS
estimate of $13.75/share plus . . . cash.*
—WALL STREET ANALYST

Wall Street analysts love to provide target prices as much as investors love to see them materialize. Most analysts, however, con-
coct target prices by slapping assumed multiples on estimates of
accounting-based earnings. As a result, they provide little if any
substance in understanding expectations.

Can the expectations investing process shed any light on target
prices? Absolutely. Here's how to decipher them.

Start by understanding the PIE for the current stock price, and
then determine the turbo trigger. Now you're ready to go.

Using the target stock price, determine how well the turbo trigger
will have to perform. You can then compare that anticipated result
with your strategic and financial analysis to assess the likelihood that
it will be achieved.

Analysts would surely be surprised by what their price targets
imply about the future financial performance of the companies they
cover. And until they move from the world of accounting to PIE, they
won't know what's in a target price.

* John Ivankoe, Rahul Krotthapalli, and Patrice Chen, "Domino's Pizza Inc: DPZ
Maintains US Momentum While International Stabilizes. Remain OW for This
COVID-Winner," *J.P. Morgan North America Equity Research*, July 16, 2020.

Much of the analytical heavy lifting is now complete. But we still
need to refine our estimate of changes in shareholder value triggered
by sales. What are the leading indicators for Domino's sales growth?

Based on the previous discussion, two leading indicators stand
out. The first is the health of franchisees. While we dwelled primarily on U.S.-based franchises, it is also important to assess the
vibrancy of Domino's international businesses, which operate
under master franchise agreements. The master franchises in eight
of Domino's ten largest markets, as measured by the number of

stores, are in the hands of companies that trade publicly. These include Jubilant FoodWorks in India, Domino's Pizza Group in the United Kingdom, and Domino's Pizza Enterprises in Australia. Profitable franchisees and good relationships with them are crucial for building a healthy ecosystem.

The second leading indicator is store growth and same-store sales. Profitable franchisees that are well supported will seek to grow, adding to Domino's top line. Strategies such as fortressing have encouraged store growth, improved franchisee economics, and fended off competition. Rather than extract more from its franchisees, Domino's has pursued a strategy of supporting their growth and financial well-being. The last chapter and this chapter discussed estimating PIE and identifying expectations opportunities. We are now ready to take the final step in the expectations investing process, which translates what we've learned from the first two steps into buy and sell decisions. It completes the journey from PIE to buy (or sell) and is the subject of the next chapter.

Essential Ideas

- If you know which expectations revisions are most important, then you improve your odds of finding high potential payoffs.
- Four building blocks constitute the foundation for identifying expectations opportunities. Historical results and PIE give us the data, and competitive strategy analysis and the expectations infrastructure give us the analytical tools.
- Identifying expectations opportunities embodies three steps:
  - o Step 1: Estimate high and low values for the sales trigger and calculate the shareholder values that result.
  - o Step 2: Select the turbo trigger.
  - o Step 3: Refine the high and low estimates of the turbo trigger and calculate the shareholder values that result.
- Beware of behavioral traps as you estimate ranges.

7

Buy, Sell, or Hold?

WE NOW TURN to the third and final step in the expectations investing process, the decision to buy, sell, or hold (figure 7.1). In this chapter, we show how to translate expectations opportunities into investment decisions by converting anticipated revisions in expectations into an expected value for a stock. We then compare the expected value with the current stock price to identify opportunities to buy or sell based on expectations mismatches. Finally, we provide specific guidelines for when to buy, sell, or hold stocks.

Expected Value Analysis

You have identified the turbo trigger for a company and formulated expectations for financial results that differ from the consensus. But that is not enough to make a confident buy or sell decision. No analysis is complete without accounting for risk. You must acknowledge that the future direction of market expectations is uncertain. Fortunately, you can use expected value analysis to

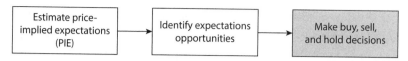

FIGURE 7.1 Expectations investing process.

deal with this uncertainty and to understand the relative attractiveness of a stock.

Expected value analysis is particularly useful for evaluating uncertain outcomes. Expected value is the weighted average value of a distribution of possible outcomes. You calculate it by multiplying the payoff for a given outcome, in this case the stock price, by the probability that the outcome occurs. Expected value is the sum of the results. Think of it as a single number that captures the value of a range of possible outcomes.[1]

How do you determine the payoffs and the probabilities? Chapter 6 described the process to estimate payoffs. You start by isolating the turbo trigger, which is usually sales, and develop a range of plausible outcomes. You then analyze the impact of those outcomes on the value factors in order to estimate the effect on the value drivers. This allows you to calculate the shareholder value for each scenario.

Estimating sensible probabilities for the scenarios is a challenge. But we can go back to the decision-making toolbox to guide our analysis.

Daniel Kahneman, winner of the Nobel Prize in economics, distinguishes between the inside and outside views.[2] When faced with a problem, most of us gather information, combine it with our own experience and input, and project an answer. That is the inside view. There is often a failure to consider a sufficiently wide range of outcomes and an unhealthy dose of optimism. This is a common mistake in the investment industry.

The outside view considers a problem as an instance of a larger reference class. This prompts you to examine the outcomes from similar past situations, or base rates, which helps to expand your frame of reference and ultimately to predict more accurately. For example, Domino's Pizza had sales of about $4.1 billion in 2020. Instead of relying solely on our bottom-up forecast, the outside view would consider the range of growth rates for all companies of that size. Historically, more than 80 percent of those companies have had a five-year sales growth rate between –5 and 15 percent, adjusted for inflation, with an average of just over 5 percent.[3]

The outside view is underutilized for two reasons. First, most of us, including investment analysts, hold our own information and input in unjustifiably high esteem. We saw this with the problem of overconfidence. Second, many investors don't have ready access to base rates so are simply unaware of the payoffs and probabilities.

Base rates are no panacea. Distributions of corporate performance, including sales growth rates, operating profit margin trends, and required rates of investment, change over time. But introducing base rates into your thinking will help you judge whether expectations appear reasonable.

You want to have a variant perception to justify the purchase or sale of a stock. A variant perception is a well-grounded view that is different from what the market reflects. This can occur either when you believe the consensus is directionally correct, but your view is more extreme, or if you have a view that is contrary to the consensus. Expected value analysis helps distinguish between the two:

- If value variability is high, which means that the range of payoffs is wide, then a stock can be attractive or unattractive even if the consensus outcome is the scenario with the highest probability.
- If value variability is low, then you must bet against the consensus to achieve superior returns.

Let's begin with high variability. Assume that the value range for a $42 stock is $10 at the low end and $90 at the high end. Say

Table 7.1
Expected value with high-variability scenarios

Stock price	Probability	Weighted value
$10	15%	$1.50
$42 (current)	50%	$21.00
$90	35%	$31.50
		$54.00 (expected value)

that you attach a 50 percent probability to the consensus value, and 15 percent and 35 percent probabilities to the low and high values, respectively. This combination of payoffs and probabilities yields an expected value of $54 per share, as table 7.1 shows. The expected value is nearly 30 percent greater than the $42 current stock price. A sufficiently wide range of value variability can signal an attractive buy or sell opportunity even if the consensus has the highest probability of being right. In this case the consensus outcome may be most likely, but the buy opportunity is the result of a high upside value of $90 per share coupled with a relatively robust 35 percent probability.

Now let's examine low variability. You'll see this with comparatively consistent companies that have stable business models. We apply the same probabilities as before, but the high value is now $55 instead of $90, and the low value is $35 instead of $10. In this case, we see that the 8 percent difference between the expected value of $45.50 and the $42 current price is insufficient to be conclusive (table 7.2). The margin of safety is too small.

Let's look at non-consensus probabilities, using the same value range as that in table 7.2, but where the consensus is not the most likely scenario. Table 7.3 shows a high-end scenario with a 70 percent probability, a low-end scenario with a 10 percent probability, and a consensus scenario with just a 20 percent probability. The expected value of $50.40 is well above the prevailing price

Table 7.2
Expected value with low-variability scenarios (consensus is most likely)

Stock price	Probability	Weighted value
$35	15%	$5.25
$42 (current)	50%	$21.00
$55	35%	<u>$19.25</u>
		$45.50 (expected value)

Table 7.3
Expected value with low-variability scenarios (non-consensus)

Stock price	Probability	Weighted value
$35	10%	$3.50
$42 (current)	20%	$8.40
$55	70%	<u>$38.50</u>
		$50.40 (expected value)

because of the high probability attached to the upside scenario. It is easy to see that non-consensus probabilities can trigger a buy or sell decision even for a company with value variability that is low. In this situation, your decision to buy or sell is a bet against the consensus estimate.

Domino's Pizza Study

Let's apply this analysis to the Domino's Pizza case study. In chapter 5 we estimated Domino's PIE based on a stock price of about $418. The analysis in chapter 6 pointed to sales as the turbo trigger with the following payoffs from the range of estimates for sales growth:

Sales growth rate			Estimated value		Change in value	
PIE	Low	High	Low	High	Low	High
7%	3%	11%	$290	$586	–30.6%	40.2%

We now examine three possibilities for what will be the most likely scenario: the consensus; non-consensus and bearish; and non-consensus and bullish.

- *The consensus.* We assume a 55 percent probability that the consensus sales growth will materialize, a 25 percent probability for the low value, and 20 percent for the high value. The expected value of $419 is close to the current stock price (table 7.4). Attaching a high probability to the consensus does not induce an obvious buy or sell decision.
- *Non-consensus and bearish.* For this scenario, we assume an 80 percent chance that the low-end value materializes, and 15 percent and 5 percent probabilities for the consensus and high-end ranges, respectively. With these revisions, the expected value decreases to $324 per share, or 22 percent below today's stock price (table 7.5). The stock is therefore a clear candidate for sale.

Table 7.4
Domino's expected value calculation (consensus)

Sales growth	Stock value	Probability	Weighted value
3%	$290	25%	$73
7%	$418	55%	$230
11%	$586	20%	$117
		100%	$419 (expected value)

Table 7.5
Domino's expected value calculation (non-consensus and bearish)

Sales growth	Stock value	Probability	Weighted value
3%	$290	80%	$232
7%	$418	15%	$63
11%	$586	5%	$29
		100%	$324 (expected value)

Table 7.6
Domino's expected value calculation (non-consensus and bullish)

Sales growth	Stock value	Probability	Weighted value
3%	$290	5%	$15
7%	$418	15%	$63
11%	$586	80%	$469
		100%	$546 (expected value)

- *Non-consensus and bullish.* Finally, let's consider a case in which you estimate a high probability that expectations will shift toward the high end of the sales growth range. Specifically, an 80 percent probability for the high value, 15 percent for the consensus, and only 5 percent for the low value lead to an expected value of $546 per share (table 7.6). In this case, the stock is a buy candidate.

Making the Decision

The Domino's case underscores the key message that a strong non-consensus point of view is essential for a buy or sell decision for companies with low value variability. As value variability increases, however, you can get clear buy or sell signals even when the consensus view is the most likely.

Note that a stock's expected value is rarely static. As payoffs and probabilities change, so too will expected values. To avoid overlooking profitable expectations mismatches, make sure to update expected value calculations whenever important new information becomes available or whenever there is a meaningful change in the stock price.

Once you establish the difference between expected value and the stock price, you are ready to consider whether to buy, sell, or hold. Specifically, look at the following three questions:

- When should I buy a stock?
- When should I sell a stock?
- How do time and taxes affect my decision?

The Buy Decision

Let's begin with the buy decision. Stated simply, you have a potential opportunity to earn an excess return whenever your estimate of expected value is greater than the stock price.[4] However, the prospect of an excess return is not itself enough to signal a genuine buying opportunity. You still must determine whether the excess return is sufficient to warrant purchase.

Your decision depends on two factors. The first is the stock price's percentage discount to expected value, or its margin of safety. The greater the discount to expected value, the higher the prospective excess return. Inversely, the higher a stock's price premium relative to its expected value, the more compelling the opportunity to sell.

The second factor is how long it will take for the market to revise its expectations. The sooner the stock price converges to the higher expected value, the greater the excess return. The longer it takes, the lower the excess return. By the same logic, when expected value is below the current stock price, the faster the price converges toward expected value, and the greater the urgency to sell the stock.

Table 7.7
Annual excess returns on stock purchases below or at expected value

		Number of years before market adjusts				
		1	2	3	4	5
	60%	70.7%	30.8%	19.7%	14.4%	11.4%
Price/expected value	80%	26.5%	12.5%	8.2%	6.1%	4.8%
	100%	0.0%	0.0%	0.0%	0.0%	0.0%

Assumes a 6 percent cost of equity capital.

Table 7.7 shows the excess returns for various combinations of the price/expected value percentages and the number of years before the market converges to expectations. Let's say you figure a stock is trading at 80 percent of its expected value. Further assume that the market will take two years to adjust its expectations to yours. You can expect to earn an annual excess return of 12.5 percentage points above the cost of capital.[5] If expectations stay the same, the stock will generate no additional excess returns.

Remember that buying opportunities do not depend on the absolute level of company performance or investor expectations, but rather on your expectations relative to price-implied expectations. A stock with high expectations can still be attractive if the company delivers results that spur investors to revise their expectations. Likewise, a stock with low expectations is no bargain if you believe that the company's prospects warrant those expectations.

Before we leave the buy decision, we urge that you avoid falling into the escalation trap. Investors tend to make choices that justify past decisions. Past investments of money or time that cannot be recovered create what economists call sunk costs. Even though investors know that sunk costs are irrelevant to current decisions, some find it hard to separate the two.

Investors manifest this behavior when they escalate their commitment to a stock by buying even more of it after it has declined. Not only are investors slow to take losses, but they often buy more of a stock just because they bought it in the past. Of course, prior investment decisions are history, and you need to base current decisions on today's expectations. You don't want to compound past mistakes. Investors who stick to the recommendation of buying stocks only when they trade at a sufficient discount to their expected value will avoid the irrational escalation trap.

How a problem or set of circumstances is presented can also affect people's decisions. Even the same problem framed in different and objectively equal ways can cause people to make different choices. One example is what Richard Thaler calls mental accounting.[6] Say that an investor buys a stock at $50 per share and it surges to $100. Many investors divide the value of the stock into two parts, the initial investment and the profit, or "house money." And many treat the original investment with caution and the house money with considerably less discipline.

This is called the house money effect, and it is not limited to individuals. Hersh Shefrin, a professor of finance, documents how the committee in charge of Santa Clara University's endowment fund succumbed to this effect. Because of strong market performance, the endowment crossed a preordained absolute level ahead of the time line that the university president set. As a result, the university took some of the house money and added riskier investment classes to its portfolio, including venture capital, hedge funds, and private placements.[7]

The Sell Decision

There are three potential reasons to sell a stock:

1. *The stock has reached your original expected value and your latest expected value estimate is lower than the stock price.* A note

of caution is in order here. Investing is a dynamic process. Expectations are a moving target that you must periodically revisit and revise as necessary. Investors who mechanistically sell shares just because they reach a target price that is out of date run the risk of sacrificing significant returns. Selling because a stock has reached its expected value makes sense only if your most recent analysis leads you to expect no further upside.

2. *Better opportunities exist.* Investors who actively manage their portfolios will ideally hold the stocks that are most attractive today. Consequently, they embark on a never-ending search for the stocks that trade at the largest discounts relative to their expected value.

The existence of stocks that promise higher risk-adjusted returns than those in the portfolio leads to the second reason to sell. This decision is different from the first one because you do not have to presume that a stock has reached its expected value to sell.

Basically, as long as you maintain your targeted level of diversification, you should consider selling a stock in your portfolio with lower upside to expected value and using the proceeds to buy a stock with higher upside to expected value. All things being equal, this will increase the expected return of the portfolio. In the next section, we will show how taxes affect your decision to sell.

3. *You have revised your expectations downward.* Sometimes even thoughtful and detailed analysis misses the mark. At other times, unanticipated events prompt you to make a material change in your expectations. A stock becomes a sell candidate if a downward revision in your expectations results in an unattractive relationship between price and expected value.

Research shows that institutional investors tend to do a better job with their buy decisions than their sell decisions. The main reason is that they pay more attention when they buy and rely more on heuristics when they sell.[8] The expectations investing framework can effectively guide choices to buy and sell.

You also need to avoid certain pitfalls when selling stocks. One example is loss aversion. Daniel Kahneman, in collaboration with another renowned psychologist, Amos Tversky, found that for most individuals a loss has about two and a half times the impact of a gain the same size.[9] In other words, people feel a lot worse about losses of a given size than they feel good about gains of similar magnitude.

There are some points to bear in mind about loss aversion. To begin, people have different natural levels of loss aversion. This influences what kind of portfolio investors build. Those who are less loss averse gravitate toward risker portfolios than those who are highly loss averse.[10]

Second, your own loss aversion coefficient may change based on your recent experience. Experiments show that people willingly turn down positive expected value propositions if they have suffered losses recently, suggesting an elevated coefficient of loss aversion.[11]

Don't forget about the confirmation trap, which we introduced in the last chapter. One technique we have found particularly useful for managing the confirmation trap is to ask questions that challenge your most cherished and firmly held beliefs about a company and its industry. Posing disconfirming questions opens your mind to alternatives that you haven't fully considered. An open mind helps improve your decision making and, ultimately, your investment track record.

The Role of Taxes

Investors sell a stock because it has reached its expected value, better opportunities exist, or expectations have been revised down. But you must also consider the role of taxes before you sell a stock for any of these reasons. Replacing a stock that is fairly valued with a stock priced below its expected value may be a bad idea after you take into account the tax consequences.[12]

Let's say you found a stock trading below its expected value and bought it for $100. One year later, the stock is trading at its expected value of $121, yielding you a handsome 15 percent excess return over the 6 percent market return for equity. Should you sell the stock?

It depends. Consider two possibilities. The first is that you hold the stock for another year and earn a cost of equity return of 6 percent. This scenario, of course, assumes that expectations don't change during the year. By the end of the second year, the stock has risen by another 6 percent, from $121 to $128.25.

Now consider a second possibility. Suppose you sell and reinvest the proceeds into another stock. What return would you have to earn on the second stock in the next year in order to justify the move? It turns out you'd have to earn about a 10 percent return, or an excess return of 4 percentage points, to make the move worth your while. That's because you would have to pay long-term capital gains taxes at a 20 percent rate on the $21 gain, or $4.20.[13] After taxes, only about $117 is available to invest in the next stock. An investment of $117 would have to earn a return of nearly 10 percent to generate the same $128.25 value at the end of the second year that you would earn holding the current stock. The required return would have to be even higher if there were transaction costs. After properly accounting for taxes and transaction costs, you are sometimes better off holding a fairly valued stock than selling it in favor of buying a new stock trading only modestly below its expected value.

Essential Ideas

- Whenever the expected value is greater than the stock price, you have an opportunity to earn an excess return.
- The magnitude of the excess return depends on how much of a discount a stock trades at relative to its expected value

and how long the market takes to revise its expectations. The greater the stock-price discount and the sooner the market revises its expectations, the greater the return.

- As an investor, the three potential reasons to sell are that a stock reaches its expected value, a more attractive stock exists, or your expectations have changed.
- Consider the important role of taxes and transaction costs before you decide to sell a stock.
- Beware of behavioral traps when you make buy or sell decisions.

8

Beyond Discounted Cash Flow

WHEN YOU APPLY the expectations investing process, you will run across companies with price-implied expectations that appear more optimistic than what the existing businesses and industry norms would lead you to anticipate. It can be a mistake to automatically conclude that expectations are too optimistic in these cases. For companies filled with uncertainty, the stock price is the sum of discounted cash flow value, representing the existing businesses, plus real options value. Real options capture the value of uncertain growth opportunities. In this chapter, we show you how to use some straightforward real options valuation techniques to augment the power of expectations investing.[1] We also introduce the notion of reflexivity, which explains how stock prices can affect business fundamentals.

The discounted cash flow model is all you need to estimate the expectations for most businesses. But many investors have come to question the model's role in valuation because it does not easily explain why some start-ups, especially those that lose money, enjoy such large market capitalizations. We believe that the discounted cash flow model is as relevant as ever if you complement it with a real options analysis for select companies.

Real options analysis is critical for start-ups that are early in their life cycles and hence have limited operating track records. Most start-ups need to invest significant sums to build infrastructure, establish brand identity, and acquire customers. Few of these companies have meaningful revenues, and fewer yet are profitable.

Real Options Defined

The real options approach applies the theory of financial options to real investments such as manufacturing plants, product line extensions, and research and development.[2] A financial option gives its owner the right, but not the obligation, to buy or sell a security at a set price. Analogously, companies that make strategic investments have the right, but not the obligation, to take advantage of these opportunities in the future.

Real options take a few forms, including the following:

- An initial investment that works out well provides management with the option to expand its commitment to the strategy. For example, a company that enters a new geographic market may build a distribution center that it can expand easily if warranted by market demand.
- Some investments can serve as a platform to extend a company's scope into related market opportunities. For example, Amazon.com started as an online bookstore but invested substantial sums to develop its customer base, brand name, and infrastructure, which allowed it to create a valuable portfolio of real options that it exercised over the subsequent decades.
- Management may begin with a relatively small trial investment and create an option to abandon the project if results

133

are unsatisfactory. Research and development spending is a good example. A company's future investment in product development often depends on specific performance targets achieved in the lab. The option to abandon research projects is valuable because the company can make investments in stages rather than all at once.

Expand, extend, and abandon options are all valuable because they give a company flexibility.

The Contingent Nature of Investment

Many investors and managers know that a project with the present value of the future cash flows equal to or less than the capital investment may still have significant value. These projects may have neutral or negative value today but might also embed flexibility that provides an additional source of value.

Flexibility adds value in two ways. First, management can defer an investment. Managers are better off paying for an investment later rather than sooner because of the time value of money. Second, the value of the project can change before the option expires. If the value goes up, the company is better off. If the value goes down, the firm is no worse off because there is no need to invest further in the project.

Traditional valuation tools, including discounted cash flow, don't value the contingent nature of an option. We want to assign value to the idea "If things go well, then we'll add some capital."[3]

The Analogy Between Real and Financial Options

There is a strong analogy between the real options to expand and extend a business and a financial call option.[4] This similarity is useful when a company has the opportunity to grow beyond its usual line of business. You should include normal growth in the discounted cash flow analysis and use the real options method to consider only the value of innovative projects that differ from the norm.

The analogy between a real option and a financial call option is imperfect but informative. The insights you'll get from real options analysis include an understanding of when a company might exercise an option, what triggers the exercise decision, and what role uncertainty plays in the value of a growth option.

Table 8.1 lists the inputs you need to value both a call option and a real option. The Black-Scholes equation is the best-known tool for valuing financial options, but all option valuation methods use these five variables:[5]

1. *Value of project, S:* the present value of the project's expected free cash flow.
2. *Cost to exercise the option, X:* the one-time incremental investment required to exercise the option at time *T.* (Note that *X* is in future dollars, and *S* is in current dollars.)
3. *Project volatility, σ:* a measure of the potential variability of the project's future value. Users refer to this variable by the Greek letter sigma.
4. *Life of option, T:* how long a company can defer an investment decision without losing the opportunity. This is usually measured in years.

Table 8.1
Mapping a call option onto an investment opportunity

Call option	Real option	Variable
Stock price	Project value	S
Exercise price	Cost of project	X
Stock price volatility	Asset volatility	σ
Option life	Option life	T
Risk-free rate	Risk-free rate	r

5. *Risk-free rate of return, r:* the interest rate on short-term government debt. We need not estimate a risk-adjusted discount rate (cost of capital) to value an option because σ fully accounts for project risk.

Here's an example of a project that has a net present value that is negative but still has real options value. A company plans to expand its distribution system in two years if demand for its products continues to grow. The company estimates that it will have to spend $40 million at that time to build a new distribution center (X = $40 million) and that the present value of the incremental free cash flow is $30 million ($S$ = $30 million) based on today's best forecast.

The project fails the net present value test if these figures are accurate because the expected benefit (S) is less than the cost (X). But the option to expand is valuable even if the company may not use it because demand could surge. Discounted cash flow is the correct valuation tool when X is not discretionary or when spending X is not contingent on some future outcome. But discounted cash flow undervalues the project when management has the flexibility to defer or reject an investment.

In this example, management can reestimate S at the end of two years and decide whether to proceed with the investment. If S is greater than X, the company will expand because the project has a positive net present value. If S is less than X, the company won't expand because the project will have a negative net present value. We need to value the flexibility to defer or reject the investment today, two years before the decision. That's why we need to value the real option.

Let's continue with our example of the distribution expansion to show how to use the five inputs in the calculation of a real option. We established that S equals $30 million, X equals $40 million, and T equals two years. Assume that σ is 50 percent per year and the risk-free rate is 0.15 percent per year. We find that the option to expand the distribution system is worth $5.4 million when we plug these inputs into an options calculator that uses the Black-Scholes formula.

We don't need to understand the intricacies of an option-pricing model to understand what fundamentally increases real options value. Value rises when the net present value $(S - X)$ increases, when we extend the time we can defer decisions (T), or when uncertainty (σ) rises.

Valuing Real Options

We can directly calculate the value of a real option using the Black-Scholes formula. But a lookup table that covers the likely range of inputs is quicker and more intuitive. Table 8.2 is an adaptation of such a table from a popular corporate finance textbook written by Professors Richard Brealey and Stewart Myers.[6]

The table reduces the five option inputs into a simple two-by-two lookup table. Panel A covers a growth option with an expiration of two years, and panel B is for an expiration of three years. Both panels show values as a percentage of S. We filled the cells of the table by repeated calculations using the Black-Scholes formula.[7] We present a range of volatilities that covers most industries.

The columns show various S/X ratios. Note that the cost to exercise, X, is at the time of decision. To calculate a company's cost today, we take the present value of X, that is, $X/(1 + r)^T$. Consequently, considering X on the basis of present value adds a modest amount to the option value as a percentage of S. Of course, a prerequisite to legitimate real options value is that a company either has financing on hand to exercise its options or has access to capital at the time of exercise.

The S/X equals 1.0 when the net present value of the project at the time of decision is zero.[8] An S/X of greater than 1.0 means that the net present value for the project at the time of decision

Table 8.2
Option value lookup table

		Panel A: Time to expiration = 2 years				
		S/X				
		0.50	0.75	1.00	1.25	1.50
	0.25	0.5%	4.8%	14.2%	25.2%	35.3%
	0.50	8.4%	18.2%	27.7%	36.2%	43.3%
Annual volatility (σ)	0.75	21.5%	32.1%	40.5%	47.2%	52.6%
	1.00	35.5%	45.2%	52.1%	57.4%	61.6%
	1.25	48.7%	56.8%	62.4%	66.5%	69.7%
		Panel B: Time to expiration = 3 years				
		S/X				
		0.50	0.75	1.00	1.25	1.50
	0.25	1.4%	7.6%	17.3%	27.6%	36.8%
	0.50	14.0%	24.5%	33.6%	41.2%	47.5%
Annual volatility (σ)	0.75	31.0%	41.1%	48.5%	54.2%	58.8%
	1.00	47.5%	55.8%	61.4%	65.6%	68.9%
	1.25	61.7%	68.0%	72.2%	75.2%	77.5%

Option values expressed as a percentage of S; $r = 0.15\%$; European option.

is positive. A ratio of less than 1.0 indicates that the project's net present value is negative.

Two key factors drive potential project value, S/X. The first is the rate of return on investment that is likely given the company's competitive position and the overall returns in the industry. The higher the assumed rate of return, the higher the S/X ratio. We also must consider the option exercise strategies of competitors.[9] Competition in many industries drives returns down to a level equal to the cost of capital (an S/X of 1.0). The second is the magnitude of past investments that may have created real options value. A company that has made substantial investments that enable options can pursue new opportunities with a lower incremental investment than can a company that hasn't.[10]

The other big driver of option value is volatility, which is the variability for the future value of S. We show a range of values for σ in the rows of table 8.2. A call option has downside protection built in. The value of an option increases as the potential value of S rises. However, option value does not drop for lower potential values of S because the company will not exercise the option once S is sufficiently low. Thus higher volatility leads to higher option value.

Volatility is often difficult to measure precisely but is an intrinsic characteristic of a project's future value. For stock options, the corresponding input is the volatility of the future stock returns, which investors can estimate based on historical stock returns or infer from traded stock options.[11]

You can reasonably use stock-price volatility as an estimate of the range of potential values for large business projects that simply expand or extend the current business model. Other projects are based on business models markedly different from the company's current model.[12] The main advice is to be sure that your estimate of volatility corresponds to the new business's range in value.

To demonstrate how to use the lookup table, let's recalculate the option to expand the distribution center. The original inputs are as follows:

S = $30 million
X = $40 million
σ = 50 percent
T = 2 years
r = 0.15 percent

In this case, the S/X ratio is 0.75 (30/40 = 0.75). Panel A in table 8.2 gives us an option value that is 18.2 percent of S, or $5.4 million (0.182 × $30 million = $5.4 million).

The lookup table provides several immediate insights about real options:

- Real option value increases as S increases relative to X (scan from left to right on the table), as volatility increases (scan from top to bottom), and as option life extends (compare panel A with panel B).
- Real options are valuable even when S is far below X. (Look at the option values under $S/X = 0.50$ and 0.75.) Discounted cash flow ignores this value and undervalues assets with embedded options.
- Real option value is bounded. Note that none of the option values in the table exceeds the value of the underlying asset, S.

Table 8.2 is small and compact but still covers a large range of volatility and potential project values. Consider the following volatility benchmarks as a rough guide for calibration:

- The average large capitalization company has annual stock-price volatility in the range of 35 to 45 percent.
- Consumer staples companies have rather low volatility of 30 to 35 percent per year.
- Information technology stocks often have annual volatility of 40 to 50 percent per year.
- Biotechnology and young technology companies have volatility as high as 50 to 100 percent per year.[13]

We constructed table 8.2 for two- and three-year options only because a company can defer investments for just a short time in competitive product markets. Options with long lives are often follow-on options that are available only if a company successfully executes the first near-term option. The value of these follow-on options is generally only a small fraction of the near-term real options value.

When to Use Real Options Analysis in Expectations Investing

Most of the literature on real options addresses corporate managers and their capital allocation decisions. Our concern is when expectations embedded in the stock price are above the industry norm and real options potentially represent part of those expectations. The goal is to use this thinking to decide whether to buy, sell, or hold individual stocks.

The first step is to evaluate companies and their stocks along two dimensions. The first is potential real options value, a judgment of whether the company is likely to have significant real options value. The second is imputed real options value, or the value that the market is already placing on any real options that might be present.

Real options values are potentially significant under the following conditions:

- There must be a high level of uncertainty, or volatility of outcomes. Industries with low volatility have little real options value. For example, consulting firms are businesses with low volatility. They find it difficult to generate huge upside surprises because they essentially sell their services by the hour.
- The management team must have the strategic vision to create, identify, evaluate, and nimbly exploit opportunities in a dynamic environment. The existence of real options doesn't guarantee that a company will capture their value. Speed and flexibility are especially important for translating real options potential into reality. Real options success is especially elusive for large companies with many layers of management that slow the decision-making process.
- The business should be a market leader. Market-leading businesses tend to get the best look at potential value-creating

opportunities to expand or extend their business. The positions of companies such as Facebook and Amazon.com provide them with growth options that are not available to their competitors. Market leaders can also preserve more of their value for themselves because they can reinforce the proprietary nature of their real options.

Let's turn now to market-imputed real options value. This is the difference between the current stock price and the discounted cash flow value driven by consensus estimates for the existing businesses.

Measuring market-imputed real options value is a straightforward extension of the expectations investing approach. Basically, you estimate price-implied expectations for the existing businesses (chapter 5) with one significant alteration: You assume a forecast period for the existing businesses instead of solving for the market-implied forecast period.

You need to do this because solving for the forecast period improperly uses the stock price, which may include real options value, to read expectations that reflect only the existing businesses. Therefore, the market-implied forecast period will always overstate the correct period for a company laden with options, and sometimes by a significant number of years.[14]

Real options value can potentially explain the difference between the market value of equity and the estimated value of existing businesses (figure 8.1). Your challenge is to determine whether the inputs to the imputed real options value are reasonable.

That there is some ambiguity between the existing business value and real options value doesn't undermine the expectations investing process. In fact, it highlights its strength because expectations investing tests the reasonableness of the sum of the existing business value and imputed real options value. Since this sum always equals the current market price, any over- or undervaluation of the

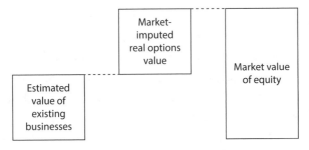

FIGURE 8.1 Imputed real options value.

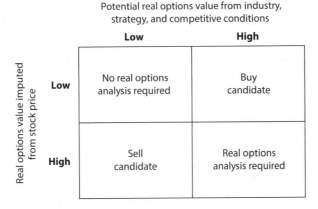

FIGURE 8.2 Potential versus imputed values for real options.

existing business value reduces or increases imputed real options value by the same amount.

We've developed a simple matrix that helps you consider when you need to introduce a real options analysis into the expectations investing process (figure 8.2). You can use the matrix to determine when the potential for real options value doesn't match the actual real options value that the stock price embeds. The matrix has four quadrants:

- *No real options analysis required (low potential/low imputed real options value).* This combination captures most established companies. All you need here is the standard expectations investing process (chapters 5 through 7).

- *Buy candidate (high potential/low imputed real options value).* In essence, you assign a higher value to real options than the market does. The stock is a buy candidate if the difference is adequate.
- *Sell candidate (low potential/high imputed real options value).* Here the reverse is true. The market values real options more highly than you do. The stock is a sell candidate when the gap is sufficiently sizable.
- *Real options analysis required (high potential/high imputed real options value).* This quadrant is where more detailed real options analysis promises the greatest potential payoff for investors. The rest of this section focuses on companies that fall into this quadrant.

Your goal is to assess the reasonableness of the project value and the total investment outlay needed to justify the imputed real options value. In other words, can the company live up to the potential implied by the stock price? To answer that question, you have to determine whether the implied scale of the company's opportunity and investments is consistent with market size, access to capital, management resources, and competition.

The Value of Real Options in Shopify, Inc.

Shopify, a commerce platform that provides merchants with the tools to start, grow, market, and manage an omni-channel retail business, offers an instructive case on the value of real options. In September 2020, Shopify was a company with large potential and the stock had imputed real options value. At the time of our analysis, it traded at $900 per share for a market capitalization of about $100 billion. The question was what combination of existing business value and real options value justified the price.

The expectations investing process analyzes real options value in four steps:

Step 1: Estimate the Potential Real Options Value

Shopify fits the bill of a company with significant potential real options value for the following reasons:

- It competes in the vibrant e-commerce market. Category growth, competitive threats, expansion opportunities, and evolving business models all contribute to uncertainty.
- The management team, led by founder and CEO Tobias Lütke, had proven adroit in creating, identifying, and exercising real options in the past. An example includes a successful entry into the fulfillment business.
- Shopify is a market leader with potential economies of scale and economies of scope. This leadership allowed it to partner advantageously with other industry heavyweights, including Facebook, Walmart, and Amazon.com.

Step 2: Estimate the Imputed Real Options Value from the Stock Price

Using historical information, *Value Line Investment Survey* forecasts, Wall Street analyst research reports, and our own assessment of Shopify's prospects for its existing businesses, we established five-year forecasts for sales growth, operating profit margin, and incremental investment. We then extended these forecasts by another five years to cover an assumed ten-year forecast period. Sales growth was the uncontested choice as the turbo value trigger.

Shopify's forecasted annual sales growth for its existing businesses was about 38 percent for the first five years and 35 percent for the second five years. Shopify would have to achieve significant market penetration to achieve these rates. Further, the discounted cash flow model assumed that it could reach an operating profit margin in the low teens.

Shopify's existing businesses were worth $800 per share based on these expectations. In other words, investors could attribute $100 of the company's $900 stock price to imputed real options value (table 8.3). The $100 per share figure translated into a little more than $11 billion in value.

Step 3: Derive the Requisite Size of the Project Value (S) and the Investment Expenditure (X)

We assumed that the appropriate S/X ratio for Shopify was 0.75, which means that Shopify's cost to exercise its strategic options was greater than the present value of its incremental free cash flows. Since we assumed that the real options would expand Shopify's current business, we used the stock's historical volatility of about 50 percent. Finally, we assumed a three-year time to maturity. Using table 8.2 (panel B), we see that the real options value is about 25 percent of S.

We can use these data to ask two vital questions: How large does the potential project value (S) have to be to justify an imputed $11 billion real options value? How large is the potential real options exercise cost (X) that justifies an $11 billion real options value?

We establish S as follows: The imputed real options value is $11 billion. The potential real options value is 25 percent of S. If imputed equals potential, then S must be about $45 billion. This suggests a $45 billion market opportunity.

Table 8.3
Shopify's imputed real options value

Stock price (September 21, 2020)	$900
Existing business value	−$800
Imputed real options value	$100 × 113 million shares = $11 billion

We establish X as follows: The imputed real options value is $11 billion. For the potential real options value to equal the imputed value, X must be equal to $60 billion if S is $45 billion and the S/X ratio is 0.75. In other words, if these numbers are accurate, investors are pricing Shopify's stock as if they believe that the company can invest $60 billion during the next three years to execute its real options.

To do a sensitivity analysis on these results, we can let S/X vary. (Note that we don't alter volatility, which is an intrinsic feature of Shopify.) For example, if we use an S/X of 1.0, both S and X equal about $34 billion.

Step 4: Assess the Reasonableness of the Numerical Results for S and X

Let's start by considering the reasonableness of the market opportunity (S). In essence, Shopify must have a $45 billion market opportunity today to justify an $11 billion imputed option value (given an annual volatility of 50 percent). Is the magnitude of this market opportunity reasonable?

Let's now assess the reasonableness of X. The $60 billion investment is substantial. Using a liberal interpretation, Shopify's investments for the prior three years were under $2 billion.

The reasonableness of S and X raised some key questions:

- What additional e-commerce activities could Shopify profitably pursue?
- What international expansion opportunities remain?
- Are there ways the company can leverage its understanding of its merchants to offer additional software or services?
- Can any company really spend this much and receive the same returns as it can on a smaller investment? Or does the scale lead to diminishing returns?

The prior version of this book used Amazon.com as the case study for real options. In fact, Amazon.com appears to have developed and exercised a substantial number of real options, including new lines of business such as Amazon Web Services.[15] But in the three-year bear market following the dot-com boom in 2000, the company's depressed stock price made it practically impossible for the company to finance the very investments that supported its real options value. In other words, the lower stock price effectively withdrew the financing that Amazon.com needed to execute its options. This underscores the vital feedback loop between stock price and business fundamentals.

Reflexivity

Investors and corporate managers widely accept that the stock price reflects expectations for a company's future financial performance. However, investors devote insufficient attention to the idea that the stock price itself can affect that performance. An important consideration in expectations investing is the feedback between a company's stock price and its business fundamentals. This feedback is particularly relevant for young companies that depend heavily on a healthy stock price.[16]

George Soros, a successful investor, calls this dynamic feedback loop reflexivity. He sums it up this way: "Stock prices are not merely passive reflections; they are active ingredients in a process in which both stock prices and the fortunes of the companies whose stocks are traded are determined."[17] We now consider the impact of reflexivity on the ability to finance growth and the ability to attract and retain key employees.

Financing Growth

Young companies, among other businesses, typically depend on equity financing. Those that consistently report results below expectations cast doubts on the viability of their business models. The ensuing slump in the stock price makes issuing new shares either unduly expensive or simply infeasible. This situation, in turn, impedes or eliminates the implementation of the company's strategies to pursue growth that create value. The stock price often continues its downward spiral as investors come to recognize the problem.

Such a spiral not only restricts a company's ability to grow but can sometimes lead to bankruptcy or a takeover at a sharply discounted price. One example of this is a handful of investment banks, including Bear Stearns and Lehman Brothers, during the financial crisis of 2008. These firms required huge amounts of capital to survive, and the declines in their stock prices meant that raising equity capital became practically impossible. Bear Stearns was sold to JP Morgan at a deeply depressed price, and Lehman Brothers filed for bankruptcy.

Many start-ups rely on acquisitions to build their businesses. And most of them fund the deals with stock, which is just another way to finance growth.[18] Poor stock price performance makes acquisitions with stock either prohibitively costly or simply nonviable. Even companies with robust stock prices should not be beguiled into thinking that issuing stock is without risk. If the market gives a thumbs-down to one acquisition by decreasing the acquirer's stock price, it will almost certainly be more circumspect about future acquisitions.

Attracting and Retaining Key Employees

Start-ups often compete in exceptionally tight labor markets and are vulnerable if they cannot offer current and prospective employees a form of stock-based compensation (SBC) that has credible prospects of suitable returns. A depressed stock price quickly shrinks the value of SBC. This drop in resources for remuneration threatens a company's current performance and prospects. Again, the spiral of decline is likely to continue as investors recognize the situation.

SBC is really two transactions in one.[19] The company sells shares, which is financing, and uses the proceeds to pay employees as compensation for service. The stock price can therefore have an impact on both the company's financial position and its ability to attract and retain talent.

A weak stock price can also undermine the confidence of other key constituents, including customers, suppliers, and potential strategic partners. This situation only serves to compound a company's woes.

Ramifications of Reflexivity

Reflexivity has several implications for expectations investors. First, investors need to ask whether they have considered reflexivity in their assessment of expectations for the company. Uncritical acceptance of a company's growth strategy without factoring in the financing risk arising from poor stock performance can contribute to disappointing investment results.

We suggest that you evaluate this outcome as the worst-case scenario when you develop a stock's expected value. The probability of this outcome depends significantly on management's vision and execution skills as well as their ability to tell a story that convinces the market that the company's business model is sound. In other words, they must persuade the market that the company deserves a high stock price even in the face of continuing operating losses.

In the final analysis, investors in start-ups that are rapidly growing and have capital constraints must recognize that these companies bear not only the normal operating risks of any company but also the risk that a stock price decline will keep the company from executing its growth strategy.

Essential Ideas

- The discounted cash flow model can understate the value of flexibility. This can lead to a misreading of price-implied expectations for a business with a lot of uncertainty.
- Real options capture the potential value of uncertain future opportunities.
- Consider both a company's potential real options value and its market-imputed real options value to determine whether a real options analysis is appropriate.
- You should incorporate reflexivity, the dynamic feedback loop from fundamentals to stock price and from stock price to fundamentals, into the expectations investing process.

9

Across the Economic Landscape

MAJOR SHIFTS IN STOCK market value, especially the rise of large technology stocks such as Apple, Amazon.com, Microsoft, and Alphabet (the parent of Google), have prompted some investors to suggest that we need new rules to understand value. We disagree emphatically. Fundamental economic principles are enduring and sufficiently robust to capture value creation across all types of companies and business models. The principles of value creation are the ties that bind all companies, which is why they are central to the expectations investing process.

We can point to a couple of issues that are behind the talk about new rules. First, traditional yardsticks such as earnings per share and price-earnings multiples are less relevant in explaining market values than they used to be.[1] A big part of the reason is that corporate spending on intangible investments, which were roughly one-half those of tangible investments in the 1970s, is now more than double that of tangible investments. As we pointed out in our discussion of how the market values stocks, this is important because intangible investments are expensed on the income statement whereas tangible investments are capitalized on the balance sheet. As a consequence, the earnings and book value of companies that invest mainly in intangible assets may appear to be lower than for companies that invest mainly in tangible assets.

But how accountants record investments does not affect the value of the company. Free cash flow is the same whether $1 million is invested in expensed knowledge or in depreciable physical assets.

Second, the characteristics of intangible assets are different from those of tangible assets. Economists have understood this for a long time. But changes in the characteristics of businesses don't change the market's fundamental valuation model.

To make this point clear, we classify businesses into three broad categories: physical, service, and knowledge. For each we highlight the distinguishing characteristics and analyze the value factors that help us identify the most likely sources of meaningful revisions in expectations. This framework shows that expectations investing is sufficiently flexible to be relevant for companies across the economic landscape.

Business Categories

Let's start by defining each category. We recognize that the activities of most companies fall into more than one of the categories. Our goal in classification is to help define the critical factors that shape cash flow and expectations revisions.

- *Physical.* For physical companies, tangible assets such as manufacturing and sales facilities, equipment, warehouses, and inventory are critical to creating value. Prominent examples include industries such as steel, auto, paper, and chemicals as well as consumer-oriented sectors such as retailers, restaurants, and lodging.

- *Service.* Service companies rely on people as the main source of advantage and generally deliver their service one-on-one. Advertising firms, consulting firms, and financial services companies fall into this category. Sales increases depend on employee growth and productivity. As a result, employee costs are typically a sizable percentage of total costs for these businesses.

- *Knowledge.* People are the main source of competitive advantage for knowledge businesses as well. But rather than tailoring services for individual customers, these businesses use intellectual capital to develop an initial product and then reproduce it repeatedly. Software, music, and pharmaceutical companies are examples. Innovation and shifting tastes mean that knowledge businesses must constantly improve existing products and create new ones.

Category Characteristics

Fundamental economic tenets apply to all businesses. But the categories have contrasting characteristics and therefore can have differing paths to expectations revisions.

Investment Triggers and Scalability

Physical businesses must add physical assets and service businesses must add people to support their growth. In other words, the need for additional capacity triggers reinvestment. This periodic need for capacity limits scalability, or the ability to sustain growth in sales at a rate faster than growth in costs. Scalability is high for knowledge companies because once developed, their goods are relatively cheap to replicate and distribute.

One example is Nasdaq, Inc., which owns and operates stock market exchanges. The company plans to migrate its markets from on-premise data centers to the on-demand public cloud in the 2020s. The public cloud vendors, including Amazon Web Services and Microsoft Azure, provide companies with computer processing and web storage. Nasdaq's technology staff had to manually add capacity to the exchange that ran on internal data centers during the surge in volume in March 2020, while operations that had already migrated to the cloud smoothly handled the additional traffic.

In discussing the transition, Nasdaq's chief technology and information officer, Brad Peterson, said, "The real benefit is the ability to scale and introduce new features." And he noted that the March 2020 episode "demonstrated how much more difficult it is to [add] capacity when you're relying on traditional infrastructure."[2]

Not all knowledge companies are highly scalable because the market embraces relatively few knowledge products. And those that the market does accept often become obsolete quickly. The perpetual threat of product obsolescence triggers new rounds of investment.

AOL and Yahoo!, two leading Internet companies from the late 1990s, provide a sobering example of obsolescence. Yahoo!'s market capitalization peaked at more than $120 billion, and it turned down a $45 billion offer from Microsoft in 2008. AOL's market capitalization reached more than $200 billion, and it was valued at $165 billion when it announced that it would merge with Time Warner in 2000. That merger is considered one of the worst deals in corporate history. Verizon, the telecommunications giant, acquired what was left of AOL in 2015 and Yahoo! in 2017 for less than $5 billion each.

Rivalry and Excludability

Physical and service businesses frequently realize a reduction in their average unit costs as sales increase. But this occurs only up to a point. Beyond that, unit costs again rise as the company bids for additional scarce inputs or gets bogged down in inefficiencies induced by size or bureaucracy. Add competition and this becomes a world of decreasing returns.

Knowledge companies are largely free from the limitations that scarce inputs impose because the nature of the goods they produce is different. The distinction is between rival and nonrival goods.[3] With a rival good, an individual's consumption or use reduces the quantity available to others. A car, a pen, and a shirt are examples. Nonrival goods, the product of knowledge companies, can be used by many people at once. The company creates an initial version of the good, often at a great cost, which it can then replicate and distribute relatively inexpensively. Software is the classic case, but any recipe or formula fits the bill. The combination of greater output and low incremental costs leads to increasing returns because use of these goods does not rely on scarce inputs.

Excludability, the ability to protect usage, is another distinction between rival and nonrival goods. Privately held physical assets are generally excludable because property rights ensure that the owners benefit from them. But knowledge goods are often nonexcludable because they are easy to transmit. That means the risk of unauthorized use is high and the developers of knowledge assets run the risk of not receiving compensation for their investment. As an example, Wang Xing, a Chinese Internet entrepreneur nicknamed "The Cloner," re-created Facebook down to the smallest details for his company Xiaonei Network. He later cloned Twitter and Groupon.[4]

The degree of excludability of knowledge assets is determined by technology and the legal system, which includes mechanisms such as patents and copyrights. Paul Romer, an economist who won the Nobel Prize for his work in this field, showed that knowledge assets can be "partially excludable," which allows a firm to profit from its investments.

Supply-Side Versus Demand-Side Economies of Scale

Supply-side economies of scale arise when a physical and service company can perform key activities at a lower cost per unit as volume increases. Importantly, supply-side economies of scale generally run into limits well before a company can dominate its market because of organizational and bureaucratic inefficiencies. Accordingly, companies in physical or service categories rarely command dominant market shares.[5]

Economies of scale for knowledge companies often rely on positive feedback, where the strong get stronger and the weak get weaker. These economies of scale are primarily determined by the demand side, not the supply side, although both sources are at play. Demand-side economies of scale exist when the value of the good or service increases as more people use it. Uber's ride-sharing business, WhatsApp's messaging system, and Yelp's restaurant reviews are instructive cases. Positive feedback often intensifies as new members join the user community because the cost of an incremental unit tends to be very low for a knowledge business. This effect can lead to winner-take-most outcomes.

Table 9.1 summarizes the characteristics of these business categories. Within categories and industries, however, companies often embrace vastly different business models, or blueprints for

Table 9.1
Primary characteristics of various business categories

	Physical	Service	Knowledge
Source of advantage	Assets	People	People
Investment trigger	Capacity	Capacity	Product obsolescence
Scalability	Low	Low	High
Products	Rival	Mixed	Nonrival
Protecting capital	Easy	Hard	Hard
Economies of scale	Supply-side	Supply-side	Demand-side

how a company seeks to create shareholder value. These differences are the result of strategic choices in areas such as product quality, technology, cost position, service, pricing, brand identification, partnerships, and distribution channels. These choices and the category characteristics shape the behavior of sales, costs, and investments in the expectations infrastructure.

Business Categories and the Value Factors

We now look at the categories through the lens of the value factors. We combine the first two value factors, volume and price and mix, for the sake of simplicity. Our goal is to show that the expectations infrastructure (figure 9.1) is sufficiently robust to capture

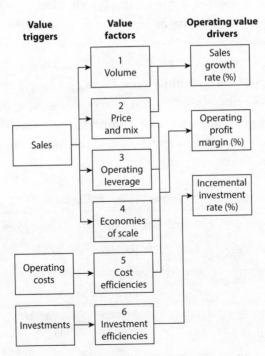

FIGURE 9.1 The expectations infrastructure.

the dynamics of all the categories and can therefore help us identify potential sources of expectations revisions.

Volume and Price and Mix

For a physical business, sales gains are tied to growth in tangible assets and the efficiency of asset utilization. Think of a traditional retail store chain. Opening more stores or reconfiguring existing stores can lead to an increase in sales growth expectations. Sales growth and physical assets move together somewhat linearly. Some retailers do better than others because of superior business models or execution skills. But sales growth ultimately relies on asset growth.

The story for service businesses is similar. Growth in the number of employees and their productivity drive sales increases. For example, a brokerage firm grows by adding new professionals and getting more production out of the professionals in place. There is a close relationship between the number of employees and the level of sales. Growth and productivity in assets and people spur sales growth revisions for both physical and service businesses.

Knowledge businesses are different. Specifically, two conditions can lead to extraordinary, and often unanticipated, sales growth for knowledge companies. The first is when a product becomes a de facto standard, such as the Microsoft Windows operating systems for desktop and laptop computers. Having one standard ensures compatibility among users and encourages developers to write complementary software applications. There is often a battle to become a standard, but once one company pulls ahead, positive feedback leads to eventual market dominance.

Second, demand tends to take off after a company forms a network that reaches critical mass when enough people use the product or service to catalyze self-sustaining growth.[6] This growth is the direct result of network effects, which exist when the value of the product or service increases as new members use it.[7] To illustrate, consider Facebook, the world's largest social networking company. In its early days, Facebook had lots of competitors, including Myspace and Friendster. Facebook needed a large enough base of members to get to critical mass and make it the network of choice. Once it reached that point, the company became attractive to advertisers. Members and advertisers flock to Facebook because that's where everyone is. Further, new members make the site more attractive for future adopters while benefiting those who are already there.

The pattern of adoption and sales growth for standard-setters follows an S-curve. Growth starts slowly at first, increases at an increasing pace, and then flattens out. This growth path is driven by demand-side economies of scale, and it has been a huge source of expectations revisions in the past and is a prime area to look for expectations revisions in the future. The winners gain the lion's share of the market, and the losers see their potential customers flock to their rival.[8]

We don't want to come across as too enthusiastic about the economics of knowledge companies. There are lots of losers for every winner in a winner-take-most market. Those losers shoulder similar investment costs as the winners but generate insufficient revenue to offset the costs. The challenge and opportunity is to separate the winners from the losers.

Sales growth is a function of volume as well as price and mix. Some physical and service companies can drive sales growth and higher operating profit margins by raising selling prices, improving their product mix, or doing both. Businesses that offer consumers greater perceived value than their competitors do, such as Apple or Gucci, can charge premium prices. Doing so affords them the opportunity to grow sales faster than costs. Further, some companies enhance their margins by improving their product mix. However, we are aware of few companies that have created long-term shareholder value solely by raising prices or improving mix.

Nevertheless, these value factors can be a short-term source of expectations revisions.

Operating Leverage

All businesses incur preproduction costs, the costs absorbed before their products or services generate sales. The significance of preproduction costs, as well as the time between the initial cost outlays and sales, varies across categories and companies. Preproduction costs are invariably sunk, however, and companies leverage them only as sales materialize.

Some physical businesses must commit large amounts of capital in advance of sales to have sufficient capacity to meet expected demand. The near-term result is unused capacity. As a company increases sales and fills its capacity, it realizes operating leverage as it spreads its preproduction costs over more units. The result is a reduced average unit cost and higher operating profit margins.

The manufacturing of solar panels is a good example. The cost of manufacturing solar panels has declined sharply in recent decades as capacity has grown. Scientists studied the sources of this change and noted the role of operating leverage when they wrote: "Larger plants realized cost savings from spreading out the costs of shared infrastructure across greater output."[9]

Most knowledge products have high up-front preproduction costs but relatively modest costs of replication and distribution. Software is the standard example. Microsoft spends billions of dollars annually developing software. But once the code is written, the company can deploy it as an update at a low cost. An increase in the number of users lowers the average cost per unit because the cost of the product is largely fixed.

Drug development is another knowledge business with high preproduction costs.[10] Medical researchers calculate that it can cost anywhere from $1.4 to $2.6 billion to move a product from development to final approval by the Food and Drug Administration. But operating leverage is significant as unit demand grows. The cost of the first pill is very high, but the marginal cost of the two billionth pill is cents on the dollar as the manufacturer absorbs preproduction costs.

Operating leverage does not expand operating profit margin indefinitely. Rather, it is a transitory phenomenon because physical and service businesses must add capacity when they run out, and knowledge businesses need to develop new products to avoid obsolescence. But operating leverage can still be an important source of expectations revisions.

Economies of Scale

Physical, service, or knowledge companies can often generate economies of scale as higher sales reduce costs per unit. Companies that successfully capture economies of scale enjoy higher operating profit margins.

One straightforward example is volume purchasing. Larger companies often pay less for their inputs, from raw materials and supplies to intangibles such as marketing and advertising services, when they purchase in bulk from their suppliers.

O'Reilly Automotive, an auto parts retailer, demonstrated the power of scale following its purchase of CSK Auto in 2008, the largest acquisition it had ever made. The company's gross margins increased from 50.1 percent in 2012 to 53.1 percent in 2019 as it tacked on about $4 billion in incremental sales. The company attributed the margin expansion to volume gains from the deal and "sourcing and finding the appropriate cost structure with our suppliers to produce parts in the right areas of the world to be the most economical."[11] In other words, O'Reilly Automotive used its size to get the best possible prices from its suppliers. Over those years, the gap between the gross margin of O'Reilly Automotive and the leading auto parts retailer, AutoZone, narrowed from 1.4 to 0.6 percentage points.

Economies of scale reflect a company's ability to perform activities at a lower cost as it operates on a larger scale. In contrast, the learning curve refers to the ability to reduce unit costs as a function of cumulative experience. Researchers have studied the learning curve for thousands of products. The data show that for the median firm, a doubling of cumulative output reduces unit costs by about 20 percent.[12] Benefits from the learning curve, therefore, generate higher operating profit margins.

A company can enjoy significant economies of scale without benefiting from the learning curve, and vice versa. But frequently the two go hand in hand. You are in a better position to appreciate past performance and anticipate expectations shifts if you understand the distinction between them. For example, if a large company lowers its costs because of scale economies, average unit costs will increase if sales subsequently decrease. If the company lowers its costs as the result of learning, unit costs may not increase as sales decrease.

The concept of economies of scope, related to economies of scale, is particularly relevant for knowledge businesses. Economies of scope exist when a company lowers its unit costs as it pursues a greater variety of activities. A significant example is spillovers in research and development, in which the ideas that arise in one research project transfer to other projects. For example, Pfizer originally developed sildenafil as a treatment for high blood pressure but found that it was more effective at inducing erections, leading to the blockbuster drug Viagra. Companies that increase the diversification of their research portfolios can often find applications for their ideas better than they could when their research portfolios were smaller.[13]

While economies of scale can be an important source of expectations revisions, our experience suggests that scale benefits often get competed away for all but the leading physical and service companies. Further, some leaders choose to pass on to their customers the benefits of scale by lowering prices to drive sales and market share. Size does matter for knowledge businesses in winner-take-most markets. The advantages of being first to scale can be substantial and often lead to meaningful expectations revisions.

Cost Efficiencies

The two value factors we just explored, operating leverage and economies of scale, depend on sales growth. In contrast, cost efficiency is about lowering costs independent of the sales level.

Companies can realize cost efficiencies in two fundamental ways. First, companies can reduce costs within various activities, which means that they do the same thing but more efficiently. For example, Kimberly-Clark, a multinational personal care corporation, launched a global restructuring program to streamline its overhead and manufacturing supply chain to reduce costs.

Kimberly-Clark forecasts that the program will generate $500 to $550 million in pretax savings over time. Specific initiatives include the layoff of 5,000 to 5,500 employees and the shuttering of ten manufacturing facilities. To achieve cost savings, the company's pretax charges to earnings are expected to be in the range of $1.7 to $1.9 billion, including cash costs of $1.5 to $1.7 billion for employee retirement and severance programs.[14]

Service companies often replace people with physical infrastructure to save costs. One example is retail banking, where the average cost per transaction has plummeted as customers spend less time interacting with bank tellers and more time using lower-cost alternatives such as automatic teller machines and mobile banking applications. These cost savings quickly show up in lower prices for services because they are available to most large financial institutions. Still, expectations opportunities exist with the adoption leaders and laggards. Companies that move first can stay ahead of the technology curve, sustain lower costs than their competition, and enjoy higher profitability than their peers.

Knowledge companies achieve cost savings primarily by reducing employee head count. Netflix, a technology company that provides media services, is a case in point. In early 2001, following the bursting of the Internet bubble, the company was worried about its financial viability and laid off about one-third of its employees to save cash. Sales continued to grow. The company's increase in "talent density," fewer but more talented employees, led to sales per employee in 2002 that were nearly 1.5 times higher than those in 2001.[15]

The second way to realize efficiency is to reconfigure the activities themselves. Changes announced in late 2008 by Advanced Micro Devices (AMD), a leading semiconductor company, are an illustration of the point. AMD had historically designed and manufactured its microprocessors. But the cost to build fabrication facilities had risen sharply over time, making vertical integration increasingly onerous. This problem was acute because AMD was smaller than the industry leader, Intel, and hence struggled to shoulder these costs.

The program launched in 2008 de-verticalized AMD's operations by separating the chip design business from the fabrication operations, which became a separate entity now called Global-Foundries. Dirk Meyer, AMD's chief executive officer, said, "This will make us a financially stronger company . . . as a result of being out from the capital expense burden we have had to bear."[16] Capital expenditures dropped from nearly $1.9 billion in 2006 to $250 million in 2011, an 85 percent decline. The company's goal was to improve its financial performance by reconfiguring its activities, independent of its sales.

Expectations opportunities may exist either if a company lowers the cost of performing its activities or reduces costs by reconfiguring the activities themselves. Investors should look for companies that have cost structures out of line with the sector, which value chain analysis can help reveal, or companies that are doing an especially good job of reducing costs without affecting businesses that create value. Cost efficiencies can be an important source of revisions in PIE for companies in all three business categories. But competition reduces the benefits of cost efficiencies, such as economies of scale, through lower selling prices and other customer benefits.

Investment Efficiencies

Physical companies that allocate capital more efficiently drive higher shareholder value.[17] A company realizes investment efficiencies when it figures out how to generate the same level of net operating profit after taxes for a smaller investment outlay, resulting in higher free cash flow for a given level of sales. The value factor for investment efficiency is particularly important for businesses that are capital intensive.

Walgreens Boots Alliance, which operates retail and wholesale pharmacy operations, is an example of a company that enhanced its working-capital efficiency through a program to revamp its logistics and replenishment systems. The initiative allowed the company to markedly improve its cash conversion cycle, a measure of how many days it takes a company to convert its investments in inventory into cash flows, from 34 days in fiscal 2011 to 3 days in fiscal 2019. Days of inventory on hand declined from 53 to 32 days. This reduced overall working-capital investment needs without compromising the company's outlook for sales and operating profit.

The world's largest restaurant chain by revenue, McDonald's, provides a classic case of how efficiency in fixed-capital investment can add value. Through standardization, global sourcing, and purchasing power, McDonald's trimmed its average U.S. unit

Table 9.2
McDonald's investment per unit

	1990	1991	1992	1993	1994
Land	$433	$433	$361	$328	$317
Building	720	608	515	482	483
Equipment	403	362	361	317	295
Average cost	$1,556	$1,403	$1,237	$1,127	$1,095

Source: McDonald's Corporation.
Note: U.S. average development costs, in thousands of dollars.

development costs significantly in the early 1990s (table 9.2). Notably, expected sales and operating profit margins from these units did not diminish. The improved efficiency translated directly into higher cash flows and shareholder value.

The pattern of investment spending is another important consideration for physical businesses. Companies that compete in cyclical industries with slow growth often tend to overspend at cyclical peaks and underspend at cyclical troughs. Investors need to monitor investment spending carefully in these businesses. Paccar, a large manufacturer of medium- and heavy-duty trucks, has been very disciplined in investing through cycles in the cyclical truck market. The company has been profitable for more than eighty years, including during the great recession of 2007–2009.

Expectations opportunities are most likely to materialize for companies that change their capital allocation discipline. For example, researchers studied thirty-seven retailers to determine the driver of total shareholder returns. They found that the companies that curtailed expansion in stores, avoiding investment that generated growth but not economic value, produced much higher returns than those that pursued growth. They argue that "curing the addiction to growth" is the key to creating shareholder value.[18]

Essential Ideas

- You do not need new rules to understand the sources of value creation across the economic landscape. The basics of expectations investing are sufficiently robust for all companies.
- Although the economics of value creation do not change, the characteristics of physical, service, and knowledge business categories vary.
- Understanding the business categories through the prism of the value factors can help you anticipate revisions in expectations.

PART III

Reading Corporate Signals and Sources of Opportunities

10

Mergers and Acquisitions

MERGERS AND ACQUISITIONS (M&A) play a prominent part in shaping the corporate landscape. Executives often risk a substantial percentage of the market capitalizations of their companies in the hope of improving their competitive positions. And unlike routine capital investments, M&A deals often strike like lightning and can change a company's strategic and financial circumstances overnight.

M&A are significant for investors for several reasons. First, M&A activity is so pervasive that sooner or later it affects a sizable portion of most stock portfolios. In the twenty-five years that ended in 2020, annual global M&A volume averaged 6 percent of stock market capitalization. Second, few corporate announcements affect the stock price as quickly or as profoundly as a major acquisition. Finally, M&A deals often create buying and selling opportunities that the shareholders of the acquiring and selling company, as well as other investors, can exploit.

This chapter explores the opportunities and risks that M&A offer to investors. We first show how an acquiring company adds value in a deal, including the key issues in evaluating synergies. We next lay out the appropriate analytical steps an expectations investor takes following the announcement of a transaction. These include assessing the deal's potential value impact, reading management signals, anticipating the stock market's initial reaction, and updating the analysis after the market's initial reaction.

How Acquiring Companies Add Value

The most widespread method that investors, investment bankers, companies, and members of the financial press use to evaluate a merger is the immediate impact on earnings per share (EPS).[1] They view accretion to earnings per share as good and dilution as bad.

The facts do not align with this fiction. Figure 10.1 shows the results of a detailed analysis of nearly 100 M&A deals done in 2015 and 2016. The columns sort the deals based on whether the company announced that the transaction would be accretive or dilutive to EPS. The column on the right reveals that managements anticipated 86 percent of the deals to be accretive to EPS.

		Anticipated EPS effect	
	Dilutive	Neutral	Accretive
Down	4	2	**45**
Neutral	3	0	15
Up	3	1	22

FIGURE 10.1 EPS effect and cumulative abnormal return. From Michael J. Mauboussin, Dan Callahan, and Darius Majd, "To Buy or Not to Buy: A Checklist for Assessing Mergers and Acquisitions," *Credit Suisse Global Financial Strategies*, February 27, 2017.

The rows show the cumulative abnormal return, the difference between the total shareholder return and the expected return, for the stock of the buyer on the day the deal is announced. A neutral reaction is defined as a gain or loss of less than 100 basis points.

The top and middle rows show that about three-quarters of the deals have a neutral or negative impact on shareholder value. The bottom row reveals that just over one-quarter of the transactions in this sample had a positive return, as they were expected to create shareholder value. Almost half of the deals were expected to add to EPS but had negative abnormal returns.

A narrow focus on a deal's impact on earnings per share is as dangerous as it is simplistic because mergers pose an additional problem on top of all the other shortcomings of earnings that we discussed in chapter 1. An M&A deal can lead to growth in earnings per share without any improvement in the operations of the two companies. In fact, the arithmetic of mergers and acquisitions can generate higher earnings per share for the acquirer even when the total earnings for the combined company are lower.

This apparent incongruity occurs when the buyer uses stock to finance the deal and its price-earnings (P/E) multiple is greater than that of the seller. In these cases, earnings per share rise but tell you absolutely nothing about value creation.

To see how this works, consider the salient statistics for the hypothetical companies Buyer Inc. and Seller Inc. Prior to the deal, Seller Inc. has 40 million shares outstanding that trade at $70 each for a market capitalization of $2.8 billion. Buyer Inc. has 50 million shares outstanding that trade at $100 and offers to exchange a new one of its shares for each share of Seller Inc. This offer of $100 is a premium of $30 over Seller Inc.'s current $70 market price. After the merger, there will be 90 million shares outstanding, Buyer Inc.'s 50 million outstanding shares plus the 40 million shares it issues to Seller Inc.'s shareholders. We assume no synergies, so the earnings of the combined entity are simply the sum of the earnings of each company.

	Buyer Inc.	Seller Inc.	Combined
Price per share	$100	$100*	
Earnings per share	$4.00	$10.00	$6.67
Price-earnings multiple	25	10	
Number of shares (millions)	50	40	90
Total earnings (millions)	$200	$400	$600

* Offer price.

Buyer Inc. currently generates $4.00 of earnings per share. However, since it gets $10.00 of earnings for each new share it issues, its earnings per share increase from $4.00 to $6.67 ($600 million of total earnings divided by 90 million combined shares) solely because its P/E is greater than that of Seller Inc. The inverse is also true: If Seller Inc. buys Buyer Inc., it suffers dilution in earnings per share because of its lower P/E. In neither case do the changes in earnings per share indicate whether or not the merger adds value.

Acquirers create value in mergers and acquisitions by investing at a rate of return greater than the cost of capital. To determine how much shareholder value the acquiring company will generate, estimate the present value of acquisition synergies and subtract the acquisition premium. The premium is the amount in excess of the seller's stand-alone value that the acquirer offers to pay. A synergy is the value that is created by additional cash flows as a result of combining two companies. The formula is simple, but generating synergies is not.[2]

Equation 10.1:

Value change from an M&A deal = Present value of synergies –
                                 Acquisition premium

An acquirer is willing to pay a premium to the seller's stand-alone value because the acquirer believes it can generate synergies that exceed that premium. Since we know the premium when a deal is announced, we need to determine whether the synergies are sufficient to add value.[3] The expectations investing process can guide this assessment.

Companies provide specific guidance on the sources and magnitude of expected synergies in nearly all deals. To assess if a deal is likely to add value, we capitalize management's after-tax synergy guidance by the cost of capital and compare it to the premium. For example, with an expected $100 million in pretax savings, a 20 percent tax rate, and an 8 percent cost of capital, capitalized after-tax synergies are worth $1 billion: [$100 million × (1 – 20%)]/8% = $1 billion. A premium below $1 billion means the buyer is expected to add value for its shareholders, and a premium above $1 billion implies the acquisition is likely to destroy value.

Evaluating Synergies

There are a few ways to judge what synergies are realistic to expect. We first turn to management. The degree to which you should believe management's estimate depends largely on its credibility. We find that management's synergy estimate is insufficient to offset the premium in many cases. For example, in July 2008 Dow Chemical (now Dow Inc.) agreed to acquire Rohm and Haas at a steep 74 percent premium. The capitalized value of the synergy, based on the company's own figures, was less than the premium. As a result, management's guidance unwittingly triggered an immediate, and warranted, 4 percent slump in its stock price.[4]

Second, research shows that managements achieve cost synergies more reliably than revenue synergies. For example, one study showed that more than one in three companies reached the cost synergies they had anticipated but fewer than one in six realized projected revenue synergies. This suggests that skepticism about revenue synergies is warranted.[5]

A third way to evaluate synergies is to use the expectations infrastructure introduced in chapter 3 and the strategic frameworks discussed in chapter 4. The expectations infrastructure is an ideal tool for assessing synergies. Logical questions arise as you go from the value triggers to the value drivers, including the following:

Sales

- Does the deal lead to a broadened product offering, expanded distribution channels, or improved geographic scope?
- Can the combined company achieve greater operating leverage from investments already made?
- Does the company have an opportunity to capture economies of scale in areas such as raw material procurement and marketing?

Costs

- Can management eliminate redundant activities, including sales, accounting, compliance, and administrative?

Investments

- Does the deal offer asset redeployment opportunities or specific capital management skills that lead to lower long-term investment needs?

Besides these potential operational synergies, an M&A deal may lead to lower taxes and financing costs. While all acquirers enter deals with the best intentions, capturing synergies is clearly a challenge. (See box, "The Acquiring Company's Burden.")

What to Do When a Deal Is Announced

Here are the questions you want to answer when an M&A deal is announced:

1. Does the deal have material economic consequences for shareholders of the buying and selling companies?
2. Is the deal opportunistic, operational, transitional, or transformational?
3. Is the buyer sending a signal by choosing to pay for the deal with stock instead of cash?
4. What is the stock market's likely initial reaction?
5. How do we update the analysis after the market's initial reaction, but prior to the deal closing?

Answers to these questions will help you identify expectations opportunities that result from merger announcements.

Assessing the Deal's Value Impact: Shareholder Value at Risk

Once companies announce a major M&A deal, both groups of shareholders, as well as other interested investors, need to evaluate how material the deal is likely to be for the shareholders involved.[6] Even if investors do not have enough information to assess the synergies confidently, they must understand the impact on each company's shareholders if the synergy expectations embedded in the premium fail to materialize. Rappaport and Sirower present two simple tools for measuring synergy risk. One is for the acquirer's shareholders and the other is for the selling company's shareholders.[7]

The first is shareholder value at risk (SVAR®), a straightforward and useful way to assess the risk of the acquirer failing to realize the value of its targeted synergy. Think of it as a "bet your company" index. It shows you what percentage of the acquiring company's value is at risk if the combination produces no synergies after the acquisition.

SVAR for a cash offer is simply the premium divided by the market value of the acquiring firm before the announcement. Here's the intuition: If there are no synergies, the premium the acquirer pays is a direct wealth transfer from its shareholders to the seller's shareholders. The larger the pledged premium, the more the acquiring company is putting its shareholders at risk.

We can also calculate SVAR by multiplying the premium percentage by the seller's market value relative to the buyer's market value (table 10.1). The greater the premium percentage that a buyer pays to the seller, and the greater the selling company's market value relative to the acquiring company's market value, the higher the SVAR. Of course, acquirers can lose even more than their premium. In those cases, SVAR underestimates risk.

Let's consider the SVAR numbers for our hypothetical deal. Buyer Inc. proposed to pay $4.0 billion ($100 per share × 40 million shares) for Seller Inc. The premium is $1.2 billion ($4.0 billion – $2.8 billion).

Table 10.1
Shareholder value at risk (SVAR) in an all-cash deal

		Market value of seller relative to acquirer			
		0.25	0.50	0.75	1.00
	20%	5.0%	10.0%	15.0%	20.0%
	30%	7.5%	15.0%	22.5%	30.0%
Premium	40%	10.0%	20.0%	30.0%	40.0%
	50%	12.5%	25.0%	37.5%	50.0%
	60%	15.0%	30.0%	45.0%	60.0%

THE ACQUIRING COMPANY'S BURDEN

A majority of the time since the 1980s, the acquirer's stock price has fallen immediately after a deal is announced.* In some of those cases the drop is just a precursor of worse to come. The market's routinely negative response to M&A announcements reflects skepticism that the acquirer will be able to maintain the original values of its businesses while achieving the synergies necessary to justify the premium. The evidence also shows that the larger the premium, the worse the price performance of the acquirer's shares. Why is the market so skeptical? Why do acquiring companies have such a difficult time creating value for their shareholders?

Many acquisitions fail simply because the terms of the deal set the expectations bar too high. Even without the acquisition premium, the prices of both the acquirer and the seller often already reflect performance improvements. For example, the current level of operating performance with no assumed improvement accounts for only about 60 percent of the stock price for nonfinancial companies in the S&P 500. The ratio is typically much lower for rapidly growing technology companies. The rest of the stock price is based on expected improvements to current performance and value-creating investments. Viewed in this light, the 30 to 40 percent premium for an acquisition just adds to expectations for significant improvement. What's more, if management diverts important resources from some businesses during the postmerger integration, declines in the businesses providing the resources can easily cancel out the performance gains in the businesses that have been bought.

Acquisitions also disappoint because competitors can commonly replicate the benefits of a deal. Competitors do not stand by idly while an acquirer attempts to generate synergies at their expense. Arguably, an acquisition should not command any premium unless it confers a sustainable competitive advantage. Indeed, acquisitions sometimes increase a company's vulnerability to competitive attack

* Jerayr Haleblian, Cynthia E. Devers, Gerry McNamara, Mason A. Carpenter, and Robert B. Davison, "Taking Stock of What We Know About Mergers and Acquisitions: A Review and Research Agenda," *Journal of Management* 35, no. 3 (June 2009): 469–502.

because the demands of integration can divert management attention. Acquisitions also create an opportunity for competitors to poach talent while organizational uncertainty is high.

Acquisitions can be a quick route to growth, but they require full payment up front for a benefit that comes down the road. Investments in research and development, capacity expansion, or marketing campaigns can often be made in stages. In acquisitions, the financial clock starts ticking on the entire investment right from the beginning. Not unreasonably, investors want to see compelling evidence of timely performance gains. If they don't, they mark the company's shares down before any integration takes place.

All too often the prices of comparable acquisitions drive the purchase price of an acquisition, rather than a rigorous assessment of where, when, and how management can accomplish real performance gains. Thus the price paid may have little to do with achievable value.

Undoing a merger that goes wrong can also be difficult and extremely expensive. Managers, with their credibility at stake, may compound the problem by throwing good money after bad in the fleeting hope that more time and money will prove them right.

Source: Alfred Rappaport and Mark L. Sirower, "Stock or Cash? The Trade-Offs for Buyers and Sellers in Mergers and Acquisitions," *Harvard Business Review* 77, no. 6 (November–December 1999): 147–158.

Buyer Inc.'s market value is $5.0 billion ($100 per share × 50 million shares). In a cash deal, Buyer Inc.'s SVAR is $1.2 billion divided by $5.0 billion, or 24 percent. Accordingly, Buyer Inc.'s shares are "at risk" of declining 24 percent if no synergies materialize.

But Buyer Inc.'s SVAR is lower if it offers Seller Inc.'s shareholders stock instead of cash because the stock deal transfers some of the risk to the selling shareholders. To calculate Buyer Inc.'s SVAR for a stock deal, you keep the premium in the numerator and divide by the combined market capitalization of Seller Inc. and Buyer Inc., including the premium. In this case, a $1.2 billion premium divided by $5.0 billion plus $4.0 billion gives us a 13.3

percent SVAR for a stock deal: $1.2 billion/($5.0 billion + $4.0 billion) = 13.3 percent. You can also determine SVAR by figuring out what percentage Buyer Inc.'s shareholders will own of the combined company and multiplying it by the all-cash SVAR. In this case, it equals 55.6 percent ($5.0 billion/[$5.0 billion + $4.0 billion]) times 24 percent, or 13.3 percent.

The magnitude of SVAR is not always obvious because deal structures vary and deal announcements usually specify terms based only on stock prices rather than premium sizes and the market values of buyers and sellers. But you know that the deal is unlikely to have a material economic impact on the buyer if SVAR is relatively small. In contrast, the transaction deserves careful analysis if SVAR is sizable.

The second tool is a variation of SVAR called premium at risk. This measure helps selling shareholders assess their risk if the synergies don't materialize. At issue for sellers is what percentage of the premium is at risk in a fixed-share offer, where the number of shares the buyer will issue is certain. The answer is the percentage of the ownership that the sellers will have in the combined company. In our example, the premium at risk for Seller Inc.'s shareholders is 44.4 percent ($4.0 billion/[$5.0 billion + $4.0 billion]).

If no synergies materialize, Seller Inc. shareholders receive the $4.0 billion purchase price minus 44.4 percent of the $1.2 billion premium, or $3.467 billion. In a no-synergy scenario, Seller Inc. shareholders receive $86.67 per share ($3.467 billion divided by 40 million) instead of the $100 per share that the deal announcement suggests.

The calculation of premium at risk is a rather conservative measure of risk because it assumes that the value of the independent businesses is safe and that only the acquisition premium is at risk. Table 10.2 presents SVAR and premium at risk for some all-stock deals in 2019 and 2020.

Premium at risk shows why a fixed-value offer is more attractive than a fixed-share offer from the seller's point of view. In a fixed-value offer, if Buyer Inc.'s stock price falls by the entire pledged

Table 10.2
Shareholder value at risk (SVAR) and premium at risk for selected stock deals announced in 2019 and 2020

Acquirer	Seller	Premium (%)	Relative market value of seller to acquirer	Cash SVAR (%)	Acquirer's proportional ownership (%)	Stock SVAR (%)	Seller's premium at risk (%)
BB&T	SunTrust	6	0.71	4	57	3	43
S&P Global	IHS Markit	5	0.45	2	68	1	32
Salesforce.com	Tableau Software	42	0.08	4	89	3	11
Analog Devices	Maxim Integrated	22	0.37	8	69	6	31
Advanced Micro Devices	Xilinx	35	0.39	10	71	7	28

Note: Values are for stock deals in 2019 and 2020.

premium during the preclosing, then Seller Inc.'s shareholders simply receive additional shares. Since Buyer Inc. completely absorbs Seller Inc.'s premium at risk, Seller Inc.'s price at closing builds in no synergy expectations. Seller Inc.'s shareholders receive not only more shares but also less risky shares. In contrast, in a fixed-share transaction, Seller Inc.'s shareholders bear their proportionate share of any decline in Buyer Inc.'s price from the announcement date on.

Assessing Deal Type

Peter Clark and Roger Mills, finance experts who focus on M&A, found that the chance of success varies based on the four types of deals they identified. Opportunistic deals, a case when a weak competitor sells to a stronger one, succeed around 90 percent of the time. Operational deals, where the operations of the buyer and seller are similar, also have an above-average likelihood of success. Transitional deals that seek to build market share have a very wide range of success rates, as buyers often have to pay hefty premiums to close those deals. Finally, transformational deals, which catapult the buyer into a different industry, rarely succeed.[8]

Reading Management Signals

An acquiring company's choice of cash or stock to pay for a deal can send a powerful signal to investors. As the SVAR analysis shows, the acquiring shareholders shoulder the entire risk and reward in a cash transaction. If the synergies do not materialize, then the acquiring shareholders alone suffer. On the other hand, if the synergies exceed the premium, they capture the entire benefit. In stock transactions, buyers and sellers share both the risk and the reward.

The decision to use cash or stock can send a signal about the acquirer's perceived risk of failing to achieve the expected synergies.

We would expect a confident acquirer to pay for the acquisition with cash so that its shareholders would not have to cede any anticipated merger gains to the selling company's shareholders. But we can expect the company to hedge its bets by offering stock if management has doubts that the deal will achieve the required level of synergies. A stock deal reduces the losses of the acquiring company's shareholders by diluting their ownership interest.

Further, management should not issue new shares if it believes that they are undervalued because doing so penalizes current shareholders. Research consistently finds that the market takes stock issuance as a sign that management, a group in a position to know about the company's long-term prospects, believes that the stock is overvalued. Ironically, the same CEOs who publicly declare their company's share price to be too low, suggesting that they should use cash to fund a deal, issue heaps of stock at that price to pay for acquisitions. Actions speak louder than words: The market responds more favorably to announcements of cash deals than to stock deals.[9]

Stock offers send two potential signals to expectations investors: that the acquiring company's management lacks confidence in the acquisition and that its shares are overvalued.[10] In principle, a company should always proceed with a cash offer if it is confident that it can successfully integrate the acquisition and believes its own shares are undervalued. A cash offer neatly resolves the valuation problem for acquirers that believe their shares trade below expected value, as well as for sellers who are uncertain about the acquiring company's true value.

However, the decision to use cash or stock is not always straightforward. For example, a company may have insufficient cash or debt capacity to make a cash offer. In such cases, management might believe that the acquisition creates value despite the additional cost of issuing undervalued shares. Or the seller may prefer to receive stock for tax reasons. Expectations investors do not treat cash or stock offers as clear signals of the acquirer's prospects.

If you own shares in a company acquired for stock, then you become a partner in the postmerger enterprise. You therefore have as much interest in realizing the synergies as do the shareholders of the acquiring company. If the expected synergies fail to materialize, or if other disappointing developments occur after the closing, you may well lose a significant portion of the premium that the buyer offered.

At the end of the day, selling shareholders should never assume that the announced value in an exchange-of-shares offer is the value they will realize before or after the closing date. Selling early does limit your exposure. But it also carries costs, because the shares of target companies generally trade below the offer price during the preclosing period to reflect the probability that the deal doesn't close.[11] Of course, shareholders who intend to wait until after the closing date to sell their shares of the merged company also have no way of knowing today what those shares will be worth in the future. Sell now, and you risk leaving money on the table. Sell later, and you risk losing money in the interim.

Anticipating the Stock Market's Initial Reaction

With the basic formula that dictates value change and the knowledge of how the financing decision affects buyers and sellers, you have all you need to anticipate the stock market's initial reaction to an M&A announcement.[12]

Start with the equation for M&A value creation (equation 10.1). Estimate the present value of synergies and calculate the premium. Take management's guidance into consideration when you assess the synergies.

Once the stock trades after the announcement, you can impute the synergies that the market expects by simply adding the change in the buyer's market value to the premium. You can then judge the reasonableness of the market's expected synergies. If it appears the market is over- or underestimating synergies, then you may have an investment opportunity.

After the Market's Initial Reaction

The final part of the M&A assessment updates the analysis after the deal is announced and the market has reacted. Such analysis enables you to judge the postannouncement attractiveness of the acquirer's and the seller's stock for cash and stock transactions.

Cash Offer. Let's start with the implications for a change in the buyer's stock price after a cash offer. Assume, for example, that immediately following the M&A announcement, Buyer Inc.'s stock price declines by 10 percent (from $100 to $90 per share). Buyer Inc.'s shareholders absorbed a portion of the SVAR with this decline. It is a sunk cost. The relevant consideration for shareholders and other investors is what to do now. You can determine the current synergy risk with a formula that updates the preannouncement SVAR:

Equation 10.2:

$$\text{Current SVAR} = \frac{\text{Premium} + \text{Postannouncement market value change}}{\text{Postannouncement market value}}$$

Substituting values for our example:

$$15.6\% = \frac{\$1.2\,\text{billion} - \$0.5\,\text{billion}}{\$4.5\,\text{billion}}$$

The numerator is the sum of the original premium and the positive or negative change in Buyer Inc.'s market value. It is the synergy bet that the postannouncement stock price implies. In this case, the numerator is the $1.2 billion premium minus the $0.5 billion market value reduction ($10 decline in stock price multiplied by 50 million shares). The $0.7 billion difference represents the synergy risk that remains for the continuing shareholders of Buyer Inc. or other investors who purchase Buyer Inc. shares at the current price.

The $0.5 billion decline also reduces Buyer Inc.'s market value in the denominator to $4.5 billion. The current SVAR of 15.6 percent is lower than the 24 percent at the time of the announcement because Buyer Inc. shareholders have already absorbed $0.5 billion of the downside risk. Thus the current SVAR reflects the remaining synergy risk for current shareholders and for investors purchasing shares at today's price. Likewise, a favorable market response to the merger announcement increases the SVAR, reflecting the greater risk borne by continuing and new shareholders.

On the other hand, the sellers in a cash transaction assume no synergy risk because all the risk is assumed by the acquiring shareholders. The seller, of course, does face the risk that the buyer will not complete the offer, which can happen for a host of reasons, including the inability to secure financing or the deal getting blocked by regulators.

Fixed-Share Offer. Let's turn to a fixed-share stock deal. Recall that the SVAR for a stock deal is the all-cash SVAR of 24 percent multiplied by the Buyer Inc.'s postmerger ownership percentage of 55.5 percent, or 13.3 percent. Assume, once again, that upon the announcement of the merger, Buyer Inc.'s stock price falls from $100 to $90 per share. Just as with the cash deal, Buyer Inc.'s shareholders have already borne part of the synergy risk because of the stock-price decline. The postannouncement SVAR thus falls to 8.6 percent, which is the postannouncement cash SVAR of 15.6 percent multiplied by the Buyer Inc.'s 55.5 percent postmerger ownership percentage.

The selling shareholders, who will own 44.5 percent of the combined company, have borne their proportionate share of the fall in Buyer Inc.'s stock price. At Buyer Inc.'s current stock price, only $0.7 billion of the $1.2 billion premium, or 58.3 percent, remains at risk. This 58.3 percent multiplied by Seller Inc.'s 44.5 percent postmerger ownership yields a premium at risk of 26 percent. Selling shareholders have to decide whether they want to risk 26 percent of their premium above and beyond the premium loss they have already sustained.

Fixed-Value Offer. Finally, let's consider the same circumstances for a fixed-value offer. If Buyer Inc.'s current $90 stock price is also the price at closing, the company will have to issue 44.4 million shares, rather than 40 million shares, to provide the selling shareholders their fixed value of $4.0 billion. Buyer Inc.'s shareholders will therefore own only 53 percent of the combined company. As Buyer Inc.'s shareholders bear the entire risk of its 10 percent postannouncement stock-price decline, the postannouncement SVAR falls to 8.2 percent, or the postannouncement cash SVAR of 15.6 percent multiplied by 53 percent postmerger ownership.

The selling shareholders in a fixed-value offer bear no price risk in the preclosing period. In fact, the more that Buyer Inc.'s stock price falls, the less synergy risk the selling shareholders assume after the closing. With a 10 percent decrease in Buyer Inc.'s stock from $100 to $90, only 58.3 percent of the premium offer ($0.7 billion of the original $1.2 billion) remains at risk. Multiplying that percentage by the selling shareholders' 47 percent stake in the combined company yields a premium at risk of 27.4 percent. Again, the question is whether the selling shareholders want to make a synergy bet with over a quarter of their premium at risk.

Mergers and acquisitions provide a fertile source of potential expectations opportunities for investors who can read management signals and assess the economic consequences of a deal. While splashy M&A announcements may fade quickly from the minds of many investors, the tools we've presented in this chapter allow you to analyze a deal's implications both upon announcement and during the postannouncement period.

Essential Ideas

- Changes in earnings per share are a poor proxy for M&A success.
- The shareholder value added by an acquiring company equals the present value of synergies minus the premium.
- Shareholder value at risk (SVAR) shows acquiring shareholders what percentage of their stock price they are betting on the success of the acquisition.
- Premium at risk shows the selling shareholders what percentage of their premium they are betting on the success of the acquisition.
- In cash acquisitions, the acquiring shareholders assume the entire synergy risk, whereas in stock transactions, the selling shareholders share it.
- A stock deal sends two potential signals to expectations investors: that management lacks confidence in the acquisition and that the acquiring company's shares are overvalued.
- Postannouncement price changes in the acquirer's stock require a recalculation of SVAR to identify possible buying and selling opportunities.

11

Share Buybacks

SINCE 2000, SHARE BUYBACKS have eclipsed dividends as the most popular way to return cash to shareholders for companies in the United States (table 11.1).[1] Share buybacks are also growing globally. Studies of a large number of share buyback programs around the world conclude that they are associated with positive, long-term excess stock returns.[2] Notwithstanding this evidence and the surge in popularity, share buybacks continue to generate a great deal of controversy and confusion.[3]

Under the right circumstances, buybacks can give expectations investors a signal to revise their expectations about a company's prospects. Indeed, share buybacks are a very effective way for managers to increase their company's share price when they have beliefs about their company's prospects that are more bullish than what the market implies. However, the signal is not always clear because buybacks serve a crosscurrent of interests, including some that do not add value for continuing shareholders.

This chapter develops guidelines for evaluating share buyback programs. We start with our primary interest, which is to identify when

190

Table 11.1
Dividends, buybacks, and total shareholder yield for S&P 500 ($ in billions)

	Dividends ($)	Buybacks ($)	Dividends + buybacks ($)	S&P 500 average market value ($)	Total shareholder yield (%)
1982	47	8	55	939	5.8
1983	50	8	58	1,118	5.1
1984	53	27	80	1,219	6.6
1985	55	40	95	1,359	7.0
1986	63	37	100	1,605	6.2
1987	65	45	110	1,723	6.4
1988	83	46	129	1,817	7.1
1989	73	42	115	2,132	5.4
1990	81	39	120	2,281	5.3
1991	82	22	104	2,510	4.1
1992	85	27	112	2,920	3.8
1993	87	34	121	3,161	3.8
1994	88	40	128	3,326	3.8
1995	103	67	170	3,967	4.3
1996	101	82	183	5,107	3.6
1997	108	119	227	6,591	3.4
1998	116	146	262	8,749	3.0
1999	138	141	279	11,129	2.5
2000	141	151	292	12,015	2.4
2001	142	132	274	11,089	2.5
2002	148	127	275	9,285	3.0
2003	161	131	292	9,197	3.2
2004	181	197	378	10,788	3.5
2005	202	349	551	11,272	4.9
2006	224	432	656	11,992	5.5
2007	246	589	836	12,799	6.5
2008	247	340	587	10,360	5.7
2009	196	138	333	8,890	3.7

(Continued)

Table 11.1 (*Continued*)
Dividends, buybacks, and total shareholder yield for S&P 500 ($ in billions)

	Dividends ($)	Buybacks ($)	Dividends + buybacks ($)	S&P 500 average market value	Total shareholder yield (%)
2010	206	299	505	10,679	4.7
2011	240	405	645	11,408	5.7
2012	281	399	680	12,064	5.6
2013	312	476	787	14,619	5.4
2014	350	553	904	17,370	5.2
2015	382	572	955	18,072	5.3
2016	397	536	934	18,584	5.0
2017	420	519	939	21,045	4.5
2018	456	806	1,263	21,924	5.8
2019	485	729	1,214	23,893	5.1
2020	480	520	1,000	29,209	3.4
				Average	4.7

Source: Standard & Poor's; J. Nellie Liang and Steven A. Sharpe, "Share Repurchases and Employee Stock Options and Their Implications for S&P 500 Share Retirements and Expected Returns," *Board of Governors of the Federal Reserve System Finance and Economics Working Paper No. 99–59*, November 1999; FactSet.

buyback announcements offer a credible signal to revise expectations. We go on to present a golden rule that we can use to evaluate all buyback programs. Finally, we apply the golden rule as a benchmark to evaluate the reasons that are most popularly cited for share buybacks.

When a company announces a share buyback program, you first must decide whether management is providing a credible signal that the market should revise its expectations. Just as expectations investors find reasons to revise their expectations, so too do corporate managers.

You need to revisit the expectations investing process (chapters 5 through 7) to assess the strength of management's signal that consensus expectations about the value drivers are too low. One of the surest ways for a company's managers to create value for continuing shareholders is to repurchase stock from shareholders who do not accept management's more optimistic view.[4]

When management signals that its stock is undervalued, you must determine which of the value drivers has expectations that are too low. We recommend revisiting the expectations infrastructure as a systematic way to uncover the likely source of the revision. As a guide, consider the following items:

- *Sales:* volume, price and mix, operating leverage, economies of scale
- *Costs:* cost efficiency
- *Investments:* working- and fixed-capital spending efficiency
- *Capital structure:* mix of debt and equity financing

Notice that we added capital structure. Companies sometimes use share buybacks to increase their financial leverage, which investors often construe favorably because it suggests confidence in future cash flows.[5] An increase in contractually obligated interest payments also limits a company's ability to reinvest excess cash at a rate below the cost of capital. So financial leverage can reduce agency costs, the misalignment of the interests of management and shareholders.[6]

But the news is not all good. A buyback program can be a negative signal in at least two cases. The first is when a buyback indicates that management has run out of value-creating projects. When a company's stock price reflects expectations for investments that create value and it decides to return cash to its shareholders rather than invest in its business, you can infer that the market's expectations for the company's opportunities are too high.[7]

The second case is when management repurchases stock to achieve announced financial targets, such as earnings per share or return on equity, that are unreliably linked to value. In many of these cases, the company turns to financial engineering to achieve its objectives because of shortfalls in operational performance.[8]

The Golden Rule of Share Buybacks

We've developed a golden rule of share buybacks that you can use as a universal yardstick for evaluating the economic attractiveness of buyback programs:

> A company should repurchase its shares only when its stock is trading below its expected value and no better investment opportunities are available.

Let's dissect the rule. The first part, "a company should repurchase its shares only when its stock is trading below its expected value," is fully consistent with the expectations investing process. In effect, management acts as a good investor when it buys its shares for a price less than the value. If management's assessment of expected value is correct, there is a wealth transfer from exiting shareholders to continuing shareholders. As a result, the expected value per share for the continuing holders increases. This point jibes with the notion that management's objective is to maximize shareholder value for its continuing shareholders.

The second part, "no better investment opportunities are available," addresses a company's priorities. Buybacks may appear attractive, but reinvesting in the business may be a better opportunity. Companies that seek to maximize value allocate capital to the investments with the highest returns first.

The golden rule also has two noteworthy corollaries:

- *The rate of return from a buyback depends on how much the market is undervaluing the stock.* If a company's shares trade below its estimated expected value and exiting shareholders are willing to sell at that price, then continuing shareholders will earn a return in excess of the cost of equity. The greater the undervaluation, the higher the return to continuing shareholders.[9] The rate of return that continuing shareholders can expect equals the cost of equity capital divided by the ratio of stock price to expected value.[10] For example, say that a company has an 8 percent cost of equity and is trading at 80 percent of expected value. Dividing 8 percent by 80 percent gives a 10 percent rate of return for the continuing shareholders. Managers and investors can compare this return to alternative investments and rank its relative attractiveness. This formula also shows that buybacks above expected value generate returns below the cost of equity.

- *A buyback can be more attractive than an investment in the business.* Management teams that seek to build long-term value understand that they should fund all attractive investments. A challenge arises when a company has no excess cash or borrowing capacity and must partially or wholly forgo value-creating investments in the business to finance a prospective share buyback. A company should consider a share buyback only when its expected return is greater than the expected return from investing in the business.[11]

We now have a way to assess management's decision to buy back stock. But even if management has all the right intentions, we must judge whether it has based its decisions on a proper understanding of the market's expectations. Beware, too, of management overconfidence. Managers almost always believe that the shares of their company are undervalued, and they rarely have a full understanding of the expectations embedded in their stock. History is littered with companies that bought back shares that they believed to be undervalued only to see business prospects deteriorate and their stocks underperform.

Let's take a moment to summarize the impact of various scenarios for returning cash to shareholders (table 11.2). In our simple example, the firm is worth $100,000, it has 1,000 shares

Table 11.2
How selling and continuing shareholders fare in different scenarios

Assumptions	Base	Scenario A: Assume buyback at $200	Scenario B: Assume buyback at $50	Assumptions	Scenario C: Assume dividend of $20
Buyback amount		$20,000	$20,000	Dividend amount	$20,000
Firm value	$100,000	$80,000	$80,000	Firm value	$80,000
Shares outstanding	1,000	1,000	1,000	Shares outstanding	1,000
Current price	$100	$200	$50	Current price	$100
Shares after buyback		900	600		
Value/share	$100	$88.89	$133.33	Value/share	$80.00
				Dividend/share	$20.00
Selling shareholders		100	400		
		$200	$50		
Value to sellers		$20,000	$20,000		
Ongoing shareholders		900	600	Ongoing shareholders	$80,000
		$88.89	$133.33	Dividends	$20,000
		$80,000	$80,000		
Total value		$100,000	$100,000	Total value	$100,000
Per share +/– sellers		$100.00	($50.00)		
Per share +/– holders		($11.11)	$33.33		

outstanding, and the stock's fair value is $100 per share ($100 = $100,000/1,000). The company decides to return $20,000 to shareholders. The first point is that the firm will be worth $80,000 following the disbursement. This is true whether the company buys back stock above or below the fair value or pays a dividend. What can vary with a buyback is how the selling and continuing shareholders fare.

Consider scenario A, where the stock is trading at $200, or twice its fair value. In this case, the sellers benefit by getting $100 per share more than fair value and the value for the ongoing shareholders drops from $100 to $89 per share ($89 = $80,000/900). Wealth is transferred from the ongoing shareholders to the sellers.

In scenario B the stock is trading at $50, or half its fair value. In this case, the sellers get one-half of fair value and the value for the ongoing shareholders increases from $100 to $133 per share ($133 = $80,000/600). Wealth is transferred from sellers to the ongoing shareholders.

In scenario C, the company pays a dividend and all shareholders are treated equally except for potential differences in the taxes they owe.

This simple example also underscores another important point. If you own the shares of a company buying back stock, doing nothing is doing something. That something is increasing your percentage ownership in the company. You can create a synthetic dividend by selling shares in proportion to the size of the buyback program, which will leave you with cash and a constant percentage of ownership.

Four Popular Motivations for Share Buybacks

We now look at the four primary reasons that companies cite for buying back their stock. In particular, we want to separate decisions that benefit continuing shareholders from those that do not, including decisions that actually harm continuing shareholders. We are looking for signals with the golden rule as our guide. We'll explain management's apparent rationale when it does violate the rule.

1. To Signal the Market That Shares Are Undervalued

To signal that shares are undervalued is the reason companies cite most often for why they buy back shares.[12] There are a number of factors that you can consider before accepting management's assessment at face value.

To start, companies can announce a buyback but not follow through. While the completion rates in the United States are typically in excess of 75 percent, they are much lower outside of the United States.[13] If a company announces a buyback but subsequently identifies attractive internal investment opportunities, not executing the buyback program makes sense. But companies can seek a cheap signal by proclaiming a program without intending to fully proceed. Investors should be mindful that an announced program is not the same as a completed program.

A company can convey the strength of a buyback signal through the method it chooses to repurchase the shares. Open-market purchases, where companies simply repurchase their own shares in the open market as would any other investor, are the most widely used by far. Open-market purchases have legal restrictions, such as a limit to the daily volume that a company can purchase, but they offer the greatest degree of flexibility.[14] On the other hand, open-market purchases convey the weakest signal of management conviction. This is especially true when the objective of the purchases is merely to offset the dilution from stock-based compensation.

In a Dutch auction, management defines the number of shares it intends to buy, an expiration date, and a price range (generally a premium to the market) within which it is willing to buy.

Shareholders may tender their shares at any price within the range. Starting at the bottom of the range, the company sums the cumulative number of shares necessary to fulfill the program. All tendering shareholders at or below the clearing price receive the clearing price for their stock.

For example, Microsoft Corporation announced a Dutch auction tender offer for $20 billion of stock in July 2006.[15] The stock was trading at $22.85 and the range was $22.50 to $24.75. Dutch auctions are generally strong signals. Shares of Microsoft rose 4.5 percent the day following the announcement.

A fixed-price tender offer is when management proposes to repurchase a set number of shares at a fixed price through an expiration date. The price is often a significant premium to the market price, and companies generally tender for a sizable percentage of the shares outstanding. Shareholders may or may not elect to tender their shares. Fixed-price tender offers are now rare, but they have historically been a powerful, positive signal to the market. This is especially true when they are financed with debt.[16]

The circumstances that surround a buyback also affect the interpretation of the signal. In particular, a few factors point to the strength of management's conviction that the shares are undervalued.[17] The first is the size of the program. All things being equal, the higher percentage of the float that a company retires, the greater management's conviction. Next is a premium to market price. Sizable premiums reflect a belief that expectations are too low as well as a willingness to act on such conviction.

Relatively high insider ownership better aligns the economic interests of managers and shareholders. As a result, managers with relatively significant equity stakes are more likely to allocate capital to create value rather than simply maximize the size of the company. In a related point, managers who do not sell any of their shares in a buyback program increase their personal bet on the success of the company. This action sends a positive message to the market.

You must decide whether management's decision-making process incorporates price-implied expectations to determine whether management is sending a credible undervaluation signal. In reality, few do. As we will see, factors that have nothing to do with creating value sometimes motivate buybacks as well.

2. To Manage Earnings per Share

When management announces a share buyback for the purpose of managing earnings per share, management actions and the golden rule of share buybacks can come into direct conflict. Earnings per share often fail to explain value because they do not account for the cost of capital and can be computed using alternative accounting methods (chapter 1). Indeed, research shows that increased earnings per share as the result of a stock repurchase do not create value for shareholders on their own.[18]

Yet management teams persist in their efforts to maximize short-term earnings per share and sometimes do so at the expense of maximizing shareholder value.[19] Why? First, they believe that the investment community mechanically and uncritically applies a multiple to current earnings to establish value. This view is questionable given the persuasive evidence that the market impounds expectations for long-term cash flows. Second, many executive compensation schemes are still partially tied to earnings targets. Although stock-based compensation dominates incentive compensation, managers sometimes forgo long-term value creation in an attempt to win the short-term earnings game.

Share buybacks facilitate earnings management in two ways. First, some buyback programs seek to offset the earnings per share dilution from stock-based compensation (SBC). In this case, companies aim to buy enough shares to keep the level of outstanding shares constant. Research shows that just over one-third of buybacks in recent years have offset potential dilution from SBC.[20]

This motivation for a buyback program has no sound financial basis. It clearly risks violating the buyback golden rule if the company's stock price is above its expected value or if better opportunities exist to invest in the business. Companies that buy back stock to offset dilution from SBC may unwittingly reduce the value of the holdings of continuing shareholders.

Companies also use share buybacks as a second way to boost earnings per share. Media outlets such as the *Wall Street Journal* repeat this supposed benefit, almost by rote, nearly every time a company announces a noteworthy buyback program. Here is a typical quote: "Buybacks reduce a company's share count, spreading the profits across fewer shares. As a result, companies can report a bigger percentage increase in per-share earnings than the profit results alone may show."[21] This statement is not even mathematically correct, let alone economically sensible.

Whether a buyback program increases or decreases earnings per share is a function of the price-earnings (P/E) multiple and either the company's forgone after-tax interest income or the after-tax cost of new debt used to finance the buyback. More specifically, a buyback adds to earnings per share when the inverse of the price-earnings multiple [$1/(P/E) = E/P$] is higher than the after-tax interest rate. A buyback reduces earnings per share when E/P is lower than the after-tax interest rate. Judging the merits of any investment, including a buyback, solely by its immediate impact on earnings per share is wrong.

Here's an example. Assume that three companies (A, B, and C) have identical $100 cash balances, operating income, tax rates, shares outstanding, and earnings per share. Only their stock prices are different (table 11.3).

We assume that each company uses its $100 cash balance to buy back its shares.[22] A, B, and C can buy ten, four, and two shares, respectively. The E/P is higher than the after-tax interest rate for A, equal for company B, and lower for C.

Table 11.3
Company comparison before buyback

	Company A	Company B	Company C
Operating income	$95	$95	$95
Interest income ($100 at 5%)	$5	$5	$5
Pretax income	$100	$100	$100
Taxes (at 20%)	$20	$20	$20
Net income	$80	$80	$80
Shares outstanding	80	80	80
Earnings per share	**$1.00**	**$1.00**	**$1.00**
Stock price	$10.00	$25.00	$50.00
P/E	10.0	25.0	50.0
E/P	10.0%	4.0%	2.0%
After-tax interest rate	4.0%	4.0%	4.0%

Accordingly, we see that earnings per share increase for company A, do not change for company B, and decline for company C (table 11.4). Note that the changes in earnings per share are completely independent of the relationship between stock price and expected value. A buyback of an overvalued stock can add to earnings per share while decreasing the value for ongoing shareholders, and a buyback of an undervalued stock can reduce earnings per share while increasing the value for ongoing shareholders.

Accretion or dilution of earnings per share has nothing to do with whether a buyback makes economic sense. This is true because the relationship between the P/E and interest income (or expense) dictates accretion or dilution, whereas the relationship between stock price and expected value dictates a buyback's economic merits.

Table 11.4
Company comparison after buyback

	Company A	Company B	Company C
Operating income	$95	$95	$95
Interest income	$0	$0	$0
Pretax income	$95	$95	$95
Taxes (at 20%)	$19	$19	$19
Net income	$76	$76	$76
Shares outstanding	70	76	78
Earnings per share	**$1.09**	**$1.00**	**$0.97**

Repurchasing overvalued shares, or refraining from buying undervalued shares because of an unfavorable impact on earnings per share, is shareholder-unfriendly finance. Similarly, it defies economic reasoning to suggest that buybacks of stocks with a high P/E are categorically bad or that buybacks of stocks with a low P/E are categorically good. Expectations investors should always focus on the gap between price and expected value and should be wary of companies that buy back their stock primarily, or solely, to boost earnings per share.

3. To Return Cash to Shareholders Efficiently

Companies that want to return cash to shareholders can pay a dividend or buy back their stock. Which method makes most sense depends on considerations such as taxes and the relationship between the stock price and the expected value.

The pattern of the percentage of companies that pay a dividend in the United States looks like a roller-coaster ride. In the late 1970s, more than 70 percent of listed firms paid a dividend. By 2000, that figure had dropped to about 23 percent, only to rebound to 36 percent in 2018.[23] Factors that explain this pattern include changes in company characteristics, the proclivity to return cash to shareholders, and the substitution of buybacks for dividends. There was an increase in the number of public companies in the two decades preceding the dot-com peak in 2000. Many of these were young companies that were not profitable and had a limited capacity to return cash to shareholders. Since 2000, the number of public companies has shrunk and the companies that are listed today are older on average. These older companies generally seek to return cash to shareholders but have in part substituted buybacks for dividends. This explains why the dividend figures have not returned to the levels of the 1970s.

Expectations investors should care about how companies return cash to shareholders because of the role of taxes and the favorable or unfavorable impact on continuing shareholders.

Let's look at taxes first. Share buybacks are a more efficient means of returning cash to taxable investors than dividends because of the ability to defer taxes. Shareholders can choose to retain rather than tender their stock and defer tax payments until they sell. Further, shareholders owe taxes solely on their capital gains. Buybacks are therefore more advantageous than dividends because of the discretionary timing for incurring the tax liability and the lower amount taxed.[24]

The relative tax efficiency of buybacks notwithstanding, expectations investors must keep in mind the golden rule of share buybacks. When the stock price exceeds its expected value, buybacks transfer value from the continuing to the selling shareholders. And even if buybacks are more tax efficient than dividends, you should always ask whether you might find better alternatives for investing the cash in the business.

4. *To Increase Financial Leverage*

Share buybacks are an effective way for underleveraged firms to increase their debt/equity ratio. Expectations investors should take note of such a development because a significant change in a company's capital structure can affect shareholder value. An appropriate level of financial leverage provides a balance between the benefits of interest-expense tax shields and the risk of financial distress.

For profitable companies, interest expense is tax deductible and therefore creates a valuable tax shield. In cases where it is reasonable to assume a permanent change in capital structure, you can estimate the value of the tax shield by capitalizing the tax savings. Simply divide the tax savings (interest expense multiplied by marginal tax rate) by the pretax cost of debt.[25]

At a certain point, the risks of financial distress outweigh the rewards of debt. A company with too much leverage may not be able to meet its contractual commitments. Financial distress is onerous, involving substantial direct costs, such as legal and administrative bankruptcy fees, and indirect costs, such as the loss of customers and suppliers. Stock buybacks that increase financial leverage can lead to a legitimate, albeit generally one-time, increase in shareholder value. But don't lose sight of the relationship between price and expected value. A company that trades above expected value can probably find less costly ways to increase financial leverage than through a buyback.

Expectations investors are always quick to note signals of potential expectations revisions. Share buybacks offer a prime source for such signals. But you must evaluate share buybacks critically, because many companies are buying back their shares for reasons that do not stand up to economic scrutiny. The golden rule of share buybacks is the most reliable guide for assessing the merits of any buyback announcement.

Essential Ideas

- Since 2000, share buybacks have eclipsed dividends as the most popular way to return cash to shareholders for companies in the United States.
- Buybacks can be a prime signal that investors need to revise expectations for a company's value drivers.
- You can rely on the following golden rule to measure all buyback announcements: A company should repurchase its shares only when its stock is trading below its expected value and when no better investment opportunities are available.
- Companies cite four primary reasons for buying back stock:

  1. To signal the market that shares are undervalued
  2. To manage earnings per share
  3. To return cash to shareholders efficiently
  4. To increase financial leverage

- Investors must critically assess what motivates management to buy back stock. Often those motivations serve interests other than those of the company's continuing shareholders.

12

Sources of Expectations Opportunities

THE PRECEDING CHAPTERS provide the tools you need for expectations investing, show you how to implement the process, and offer frameworks to assess management's major capital allocation decisions. You have the foundation you need to look for expectations mismatches that are the source of excess returns.

Our decades of teaching these ideas to executives, investors, and students have provided us with a sense of the sources of expectations opportunities. Here are eight cases where the expectations investing process may improve the odds of gaining a profitable insight.

1. Using Probabilities for Opportunity, Feedback, and a Prompt

Expectations investing is a process that guides the search for gaps between price and expected value. A thoughtful expected value analysis requires good inputs for the probabilities of various scenarios for the value trigger, typically sales growth, and outcomes that you can calculate using the expectations infrastructure.

An opportunity for an expectations revision can arise when you believe that the market fails to recognize an outcome or places a probability on it that is too high or low. Considering outcomes and probabilities is a skill that you can cultivate with the proper tools and feedback.

Overprecision, excessive confidence that you know how the future will unfold, is a common mistake in setting scenarios and their probabilities. We discussed this in chapter 6. The market also fails to reflect the proper probability of particular outcomes from time to time. The goal is to come up with probabilities for the scenarios that are correctly calibrated. Doing so creates the opportunity to learn through feedback and provides a natural prompt to revisit expectations.

Gary Klein, a psychologist, came up with the idea of a premortem.[1] Most people are familiar with a postmortem, where you learn from mistakes in the past in order to make better decisions in the present. A premortem launches you into the future and prompts you to think about the reasons that a current decision could go wrong.

For example, a company considering an acquisition might assemble a group of senior leaders, assume they proceeded with the deal, and then have each person independently write a newspaper article dated a year from now with explanations for why the deal failed. The power of a premortem is that it counters overprecision by opening the mind to a wide range of outcomes.

In considering the likelihood of various scenarios, it is essential to assign numerical probabilities rather than use words. For instance, instead of "there's a real possibility that sales growth will exceed 10 percent over the next year," you would say, "there's a 70 percent probability that sales growth will exceed 10 percent over the next year." There are a few advantages of using probabilities in place of words.

The first is that people assign different probabilities to the same common words or phrases.[2] For example, thousands of people were asked to attach a numerical probability to the term *real possibility*, and their responses were in a range between 25 and 85 percent.

Vague verbiage can present a problem when communicating with others and offers you psychological cover no matter what happens. If sales growth does exceed 10 percent in the next year, you can say, "I told you it was a real possibility." If it doesn't, you can say, "I told you it was only a real possibility."

Keeping track of probabilistic forecasts and the relevant outcomes also allows for accurate feedback. Success as an active investor ultimately comes down to earning excess returns. But stock-price movements are notoriously noisy. Breaking down an investment case into probabilities and outcomes allows you to keep score of your assessments.

The objective is to be as well calibrated as possible. Calibration measures the difference between the probabilities you assign and the actual outcomes. You can count the cases when someone who is perfectly calibrated says something happens 70 percent of the time, and you'll find that it indeed happens 7 in 10 times. Research shows that keeping track of those probabilities and outcomes provides valuable feedback that allows forecasters to become better calibrated over time.[3]

Expectations mismatches, the difference between price and expected value, are the basis for the decision to buy or sell a stock. A mismatch means that your analysis leads you to believe something about a company's prospects that are not reflected in the stock price. That variant perception is based on the probabilities and outcomes you develop.

You should pass certain signposts, affirmations that you are on the right path, if your thesis unfolds as you anticipate. If you believe sales growth will exceed 10 percent over the year with a 70 percent probability, you should see that rate of growth with that frequency. That would indicate that your thesis is on track.

Signposts also create a clear prompt to revisit your thesis in cases when results differ from what you anticipated. Recall that one of the reasons to exit a position is if your analysis misses the mark. This will happen. The key is to deal with the situation honestly and to allocate your time to more promising opportunities.

2. Assessing Macroeconomic Shocks

Philip Tetlock, a professor of psychology at the University of Pennsylvania, tracked thousands of expert forecasts of political, social, and economic outcomes and wrote about them in his book, *Expert Political Judgment*.[4] Tetlock discovered that the predictions of these experts were not much better than what you would have expected by chance and were only slightly better than the forecasts of casually informed nonexperts. He also found that the confidence of the experts exceeded their capability.

Investors who use the expectations investing process recognize that they are unlikely to be able to forecast better than the experts. As a result, they are open to considering a range of outcomes driven by macroeconomic shocks. These include sharp changes in the price of key commodities such as oil, natural disasters such as hurricanes and earthquakes, inflation, geopolitical turmoil, and changes in central bank policy.

We introduced an industry map in chapter 4 that provides expectations investors with an understanding of industry dynamics and a way to assess present and future profitability. You can use it to measure the impact of an economic shock on the economy, the industry, and the company you are studying. You can incorporate these potential forecasts into scenario analysis. Monte Carlo methods, which allow you to simulate many possible outcomes, are a useful way to consider the impact of economic shocks.

Use the expectations infrastructure, described in chapter 3, to assess how macro changes will affect the three value triggers:

sales, operating costs, and investments. Then carefully consider how those triggers will shape the six value factors: volume, price and mix, operating leverage, economies of scale, cost efficiencies, and investment efficiencies. The value factors ultimately lead to the value drivers—sales growth, operating profit margins, and incremental investment rate—that allow you to assess expectations.

The coronavirus 2019 pandemic, which swept across the world in 2020, is a good illustration of how to consider the impact of a macro shock. Researchers examined the market's reaction to the pandemic over three early periods. Incubation, from the beginning of 2020 through January 17, was the first. Next was the outbreak phase, which was January 20 through February 21. The final phase, fever, ran from February 24 through March 20 and ended at the stock market's low for the year.[5]

Stocks in the food industry and food and drug retailing had poor returns during the incubation and outbreak periods but outperformed sharply in the fever phase as the market revised its expectations to acknowledge the magnitude of the crisis. Hotel, restaurant, and leisure stocks realized neutral relative returns in the early periods but dropped precipitously as the market reflected the calamity of the pandemic. All returns are adjusted for risk.

The researchers also found that the stocks of companies with high levels of debt had worse returns in the fever period than those with low levels of debt. Businesses with high fixed costs, such as hotels and airlines, also tend to have above-average levels of financial leverage. Many of these companies faced existential threats. The stocks of companies with substantial cash balances, on the other hand, performed well because they were positioned to weather the storm.

No one knows what the future holds, but the expectations investing process provides the tools you need to consider the impact of a wide range of macroeconomic shocks.

3. Evaluating Changes in Senior Management

A change in management, especially following poor stock-price performance, is a good time to revisit expectations.[6] Naturally, management changes can be good, bad, or indifferent. But they offer an opportunity to reassess a company's operational performance, strategic positioning, and capital allocation policies in a search for potential revisions in expectations.

In his book *The Outsiders*, Will Thorndike, the founder of a private equity firm, tells the stories of eight CEOs who delivered excellent total shareholder returns during their tenure.[7] In other words, expectations were very low when each of the CEOs took over. Common attributes among this group included an emphasis on capital allocation, independent thinking, and a focus on creating long-term value. They also tended to be analytical and maintained relatively low profiles with the media. The lesson is to assess new management teams to identify potential changes that might reset the market's expectations.

Transitions following periods of weakness or strength in business results are particularly noteworthy. For example, David Cote took over the industrial conglomerate Honeywell in February 2002. Honeywell had struck a deal to be acquired by General Electric (GE), a larger industrial conglomerate, for $55 a share in late 2000, but the deal was scuttled in July 2001 as the result of regulatory concerns. The combination of the failed transaction and the recession that year pushed the stock down to $35 by the time that Cote took over. His operational, strategic, and financial initiatives resulted in a 700-basis-point improvement in operating profit margin, propelling the stock to handily outperform the S&P 500 during his fifteen-year tenure.[8]

Handing over the reins at the top can also be an opportunity to revisit expectations.[9] When Jack Welch became CEO of GE in 1981, the stock had declined by one-quarter over the past decade. He moved quickly to realign the company's portfolio of businesses and to cut costs. The company also became known for meeting or beating Wall Street's quarterly earnings estimates, often doing so through accounting tricks. Welch's handpicked successor, Jeff Immelt, took over in September 2001. GE's stock returns were nearly fourfold those of the S&P 500 during Welch's tenure, and expectations were high.

The combination of the high expectations embedded in GE's stock price and poor capital allocation led to a total shareholder return for GE's stock of 8 percent over Immelt's tenure. The S&P 500's total shareholder return was 214 percent over the same period.

Using an executive's past to project performance in a new role can be a challenge. Boris Groysberg, a professor of organizational behavior at Harvard Business School, studied the performance of stars after they join new organizations. Executives who left GE are an illuminating case.[10] GE, which had its own executive development center in Crotonville, New York, was known for providing its brightest managers with great training. Groysberg and his collaborators looked at twenty executives that other firms hired from GE to be their CEO or chairman in the twelve years that ended in 2001. Half of those managers went to businesses that were similar to GE. Their skills transferred and the companies fared well. The other ten went to companies that were different from GE. Those companies floundered. Notwithstanding GE's outstanding reputation for training executives, there was a fundamental skills mismatch that stymied their success.

4. Judging Stock Splits, Dividends, Stock Buybacks, and Stock Issuance

In the summer of 2020, there were stock split announcements from two high-profile companies, Apple Inc. (four-for-one) and Tesla, Inc. (five-for-one). Both stocks immediately rose sharply. This makes little sense if the market can do math because a stock split simply divides shareholder value by more shares outstanding. A pizza cut in eight slices provides no more to eat than the same pizza cut in four slices.

Recent studies show that stock splits do lead to excess shareholder returns, albeit the effect tends to be short-lived.[11] There are a couple of theories about why this might be so. The first, which ties together the concepts in this section, is that stock splits are a signal of confidence by the board of directors. The other is that stock splits create more liquidity for the shares. Illiquid stocks require a premium expected return to compensate holders, so increasing liquidity lowers that premium and increases value.[12] We do not, however, recommend focusing on stock splits as a source of meaningful expectations gaps.

Dividends and share buybacks are identical under stringent assumptions about taxes, timing, shareholder reinvestment, and stock price. What is not identical is the attitude of executives toward dividends versus buybacks. They deem maintaining the dividend to be as important as capital expenditures but often view buybacks as a means to deploy residual cash after they have funded all appropriate investments.[13] We see this in the data. The series of aggregate dividend payouts is relatively smooth as compared to the uneven pattern for buybacks.

Dividends can also provide signals for expectations investors. The first signal is that dividend changes are positively related to future profitability.[14] This makes sense if the board of directors considers dividend payments as a quasi-contract because they would make such a commitment only if they had confidence in future cash flows. But the evidence for this signal is mixed.

Dividends may offer a signal about future volatility in cash flow as well.[15] Initiations or dividend increases tend to precede a reduction in cash flow volatility, and dividend cuts commonly anticipate increased volatility. Changes in volatility can affect the cost of capital and hence the stock price. While academics have documented these signals from dividends, they are rarely strong enough to lead to a revision in expectations that is sufficiently large to spur action.

Buying and issuing stock can also provide investors with a reason to revisit expectations. We noted in chapter 11 that buying back undervalued stock adds value for continuing shareholders. Chapter 10 pointed out that corporate buyers that fund an acquisition by issuing stock fare worse on average than buyers that do deals with cash.

Taking a step back, academic research makes this point more broadly. Issuing stock tends to be associated with poor subsequent total shareholder returns, and buying back stock leads to above-average returns.[16] Expectations investors benefit from understanding this pattern even though the high-level findings do not apply to any particular company in any specific instance.

Indeed, a broader conclusion from the study of capital allocation is that high asset growth rates are a strong predictor of future low abnormal returns and vice versa.[17] This makes sense because it is difficult for a company to spend a large sum on investments, which asset growth captures, and earn a return substantially above the cost of capital. Just as it is hard for a portfolio manager to find attractive stocks to buy when her portfolio size swells, it is hard for an executive to allocate large sums of capital.

5. Estimating the Impact of Lawsuits

Corporate actions can sometimes give rise to a lawsuit. High-profile cases include BP plc, a British oil and gas company, following the Deepwater Horizon oil spill in 2010; Volkswagen, a German automobile producer, after it falsely disclosed low emissions for certain vehicles; and Enron, an American energy company that defrauded shareholders prior to filing for bankruptcy.

The research shows a negative reaction in the stock price of companies that are sued.[18] The decline in value can come from a couple of sources. Losing a lawsuit may result in monetary penalties. For example, BP ultimately paid about $20 billion to settle lawsuits, above and beyond fines and cleanup costs.[19] Note, though, that the defendants rarely end up paying the headline sum demanded by the plaintiff, and many companies have insurance that can offset some of the cost.

These penalties increase the liabilities that you need to subtract from corporate value to calculate shareholder value. In some cases, they can tip a company into bankruptcy. For example, Purdue Pharma, maker of the opioid OxyContin, filed for bankruptcy after a multibillion-dollar settlement with states that accused the company of playing a pivotal role in the opioid crisis.

Stock-price underperformance can also come from lower future cash flows, especially if the action triggering the lawsuit causes reputational damage. For instance, Volkswagen was barred from selling diesel automobiles in the United States for a time after the revelation of fraudulent claims for emissions.

Expectations investors may come to a view that the market is over- or underestimating the cost associated with a lawsuit based on legal analysis. Integrating the analysis into the expectations investing process will yield a more confident assessment of the opportunity.

6. Capturing External Changes: Subsidies, Tariffs, Quotas, and Regulations

Companies adopt strategies in the pursuit of a competitive advantage. These advantages include the ability to produce a good or service at a lower price than competitors and the ability to price a good or service at a premium to the market average. But advantages can also shift as the result of government interventions in the form of subsidies, tariffs, quotas, and regulations. These interventions are built into the business landscape. For example, the code of federal regulations in the United States has more than 180,000 pages.[20] Changes in regulatory interventions can reshape expectations.

One case in point is threatened or imposed tariffs, a tax on a particular import. From 2017 through 2020, the United States threatened or imposed tariffs on goods from China, Canada, Mexico, Brazil, and France. In many of these cases the targeted country retaliated with tariffs of its own, stunting trade. In early December 2019, for instance, the United States announced an increase in tariffs on steel and aluminum imports from Brazil and Argentina. This took the market by surprise and led to sharp gains in the stock prices of U.S. steel producers.

In November 2020 the voters of California weighed in on Proposition 22. Passing the proposition would allow rideshare and delivery companies to keep classifying their drivers as independent contractors. Defeating the proposition would mean that the companies would have to hire the drivers as employees, which is substantially costlier. Contract workers also have a lot more flexibility than employees do, including in selecting which company they would like to work for and what hours they would like to work. The stocks of the large rideshare and delivery companies, including Uber and Lyft, rose sharply on the news that Proposition 22 passed.

The imposition of regulation on an industry can benefit the larger incumbents because the cost of adherence serves as a barrier to entry. Consider the regulation adopted by the European Union (EU) to protect data and privacy, called General Data Protection Regulation (GDPR), which was enforceable starting in May 2018.

The costs for EU and U.S. companies to comply with the regulations are estimated to be in excess of $280 billion. While the regulation meant to limit the power of technology giants such as Alphabet Inc., the parent of Google, many smaller companies lacked the resources to fulfill the GDPR's requirements. As a result, Google gained market share at the expense of its competitors.[21]

Similar to macroeconomic shocks, government interventions can be difficult to predict. However, investors can consider them in their scenario analysis, using the expectations infrastructure to quantify the potential impact on shareholder value.

7. Measuring the Impact of Divestitures

Another way that companies try to create value is through divestitures, including the sale of divisions and spin-offs. Common motivations for a divestiture include when a company perceives the value of an asset to be higher for another owner and when a divestiture allows the parent company to be more focused.

Research has shown that a relatively small percentage of assets create the majority of the value for most companies.[22] Executives who are astute capital allocators recognize that businesses or assets that do not earn the cost of capital may be worth more to a strategic or financial buyer.

When a company divests a business with low returns and receives a sum in excess of what the operation is worth as part of the firm, there is addition by subtraction. The firm adds value as it subtracts from its size.

Chapter 10 showed that acquirers struggle to create value in mergers and acquisitions (M&A) because the premium they pledge is often bigger than the synergies they are likely to realize. M&A create value in the aggregate, but it is common to see a wealth transfer from the shareholders of the buyer to those of the seller. In other words, in general it is better to be a seller than a buyer.

The executives of most companies have an incentive to grow and are therefore reticent to shrink. And asset sales are sometimes forced because of a company's poor performance or precarious financial position. But the research on divestitures concludes that they add value on average.[23] Analysis also shows that spin-offs, when a company distributes shares of a wholly owned subsidiary to its shareholders on a pro rata and tax-free basis, create value for the business spun off as well as the parent.

There can be a great opportunity to create value through divestitures when a CEO who is a skillful capital allocator assumes leadership of a company with underperforming assets. This combination creates ripe conditions for expectations revisions.

8. Coping with Extreme Stock-Price Moves

From time to time you might see a sharp loss or gain for a stock you own. These losses or gains may be precipitated by an earnings announcement, where the real news is often in the forward guidance, or by surprising news such as the resignation of a key executive.

These material moves can trigger a strong emotional response. If you hold a stock of a company that sees its shares plummet, you may feel upset, frustrated, or even misled. Studies of decision making have taught us that it is hard to make good decisions when emotionally aroused. As a result, it can be difficult to stick to the discipline of expectations investing under these conditions.

Checklists can help you make good decisions. There are two kinds of checklists. With the first, you do the tasks and then pause to confirm that you have completed them thoroughly. For example, this is what airplane pilots do before takeoff. Such a checklist is helpful for the normal expectations investing process.

The second kind applies during emergencies or stressful situations. Here you read the checklist and do what it says. For instance, if an airplane engine fails during flight, a pilot consults such a checklist. This is the checklist we want to create to guide decisions following a large stock-price move.

Let's start with price declines. We looked at 5,400 cases, over twenty-five years, of when a company's stock dropped 10 percentage points relative to the S&P 500 in one day. We sorted these declines into earnings and nonearnings events.[24] Then we measured three factors prior to the decline: momentum, valuation, and quality.[25] Adding factors shrinks the sample sizes of the reference classes but increases the similarity between observations. Finally, we calculated the average excess returns for the subsequent 30, 60, and 90 trading days.

We conducted a similar analysis for 6,800 one-day relative price gains of 10 percentage points or more over a quarter-century. Gains are trickier than losses because we have to remove increases as the result of acquisitions.[26] For price declines and price gains, buy signals were more common for stocks with poor momentum but attractive valuations, and sell signals were more common for stocks that had positive momentum and a valuation that reflected high expectations.

That said, this analysis provides a naïve default assumption for the average return for the appropriate category. The average return tells only a part of the story because each category has a distribution of returns, which means that the excess returns in any particular instance may be different from the average. But base rates help quantify the likelihood of outcomes and provide guidance as to whether to buy, sell, or hold the stock.

Essential Ideas

- You need to be prepared to deal with macroeconomic shocks and other external changes such as subsidies, tariffs, quotas, and regulations. The expectations infrastructure can help guide that analysis. You can use base rates to evaluate large stock-price moves.
- Announcements of such things as stock splits, changes in dividend policy, or stock issuance or stock buyback can provide signals that you should revise expectations.
- Management changes can be substantial catalysts for expectations revisions, especially if the new leadership focuses on value creation rather than simply growth.

Notes

1. The Case for Expectations Investing

1. Warren E. Buffett, "Buy American. I Am." *New York Times*, October 16, 2008, https://www.nytimes.com/2008/10/17/opinion/17buffett.html?_r=0.

2. We assume that investors have already chosen investment policies that reflect their risk tolerance, which determines the level of equity exposure and the degree of diversification in the equity sector.

3. Berlinda Liu and Gaurav Sinha, "SPIVA® U.S. Scorecard," *S&P Dow Jones Indices Research*, September 21, 2020.

4. This idea is called the paradox of skill. See Michael J. Mauboussin, *The Success Equation: Untangling Skill and Luck in Business, Sports, and Investing* (Boston: Harvard Business Review Press, 2012), 53–58.

5. On average, active managers earn lower returns than their benchmarks largely as a consequence of fees. See William F. Sharpe, "The Arithmetic of Active Management," *Financial Analysts' Journal* 47, no. 1 (January–February 1991): 7–9.

6. John C. Bogle, *Common Sense on Mutual Funds: New Imperatives for the Intelligent Investor* (New York: Wiley, 1999), 92.

7. Ben Johnson and Gabrielle Dibenedetto, "2019 U.S. Fund Fee Study: Marking Nearly Two Decades of Falling Fees," *Morningstar Manager Research*, June 2020.

8. Berkshire Hathaway Annual Report, 2000, 13, https://www.berkshire hathaway.com/letters/2000pdf.pdf.

9. Jack L. Treynor, "Long-Term Investing," *Financial Analysts' Journal* 32, no. 3 (May–June 1976): 56.

10. John Burr Williams, *The Theory of Investment Value* (Cambridge, MA: Harvard University Press, 1938), 186–191.

11. Research studies confirm that announced changes in accounting methods that alter reported earnings, but not cash flows, don't affect the stock price.

12. Investment Company Institute, *Investment Company Fact Book: A Review of Trends and Activities in the Investment Company Industry*, 61st ed., May, 2021, https://www.ici.org/system/files/2021-05/2021_factbook.pdf.

13. Alfred Rappaport, "CFOs and Strategists: Forging a Common Framework," *Harvard Business Review* 70, no. 3 (May–June 1992): 87.

14. John R. Graham, Campbell R. Harvey, and Shiva Rajgopal, "Value Destruction and Financial Reporting Decisions," *Financial Analysts' Journal* 62, no. 6 (November–December 2006): 27–39.

15. Frank J. Fabozzi, Sergio M. Focardi, and Caroline Jonas, *Equity Valuation: Science, Art, or Craft?* (Charlottesville, VA: CFA Institute Research Foundation, 2017). Based on nearly two thousand respondents to the 2015 CFA Institute Study.

2. How the Market Values Stocks

1. Suppose someone offers you a contract specifying that you will receive $10,000 one year from today. What is the most you should pay for this contract today? The answer, of course, depends on the rate of return that you can expect to earn over the next year. If the one-year interest rate for investments of comparable risk is 5 percent, then you shouldn't pay more than the dollar amount, which, when compounded at a 5 percent rate, equals $10,000 by the end of the year. Since you know next year's cash flow ($10,000) and the discount rate (5 percent), you can easily determine the present value or maximum you should pay of $9,524:

$$\text{Present value} \times (1 + \text{rate of return}) = \text{Future value}$$
$$\text{Present value} (1.05) = \$10,000$$
$$\text{Present value} = \$9,524$$

2. Neil Barsky, "Empire State Building to Be Sold to a Peter Grace Family Member," *New York Times*, October 31, 1991.

3. John C. Bogle, *John Bogle on Investing: The First 50 Years* (New York: McGraw-Hill, 2000), 53.

4. Why do we add back amortization of acquired intangibles but not depreciation even though both are noncash charges? Depreciation captures wear and tear on physical assets and hence is appropriately considered an operating expense. Amortization of acquired intangibles reflects different accounting. The investments a company makes in intangible assets such as customer acquisition or brand building are expensed, not capitalized. Only acquired intangible assets are amortized. Those acquired intangible assets also lose value, but because a company's investment to replenish those assets is expensed, we don't want to penalize the company twice (first through amortization and second through investment in intangibles).

Why do we add back the embedded interest expense from operating lease expense? Starting in early 2019, most companies, whether they report under U.S. Generally Accepted Accounting Principles (GAAP) or International Financial Reporting Standards (IFRS), must reflect most leases on the balance sheet. Under GAAP, the entire lease expense, including embedded interest, is still expensed. Under IFRS, the lease payments are appropriately allocated to depreciation and interest expense. To be consistent, you need to add embedded interest expense back to operating income in order to calculate NOPAT.

5. You can generally estimate the adjustment between book and cash taxes by looking at the change in accumulated deferred taxes on the balance sheet (the net of deferred tax assets and deferred tax liabilities).

6. Note that we did not adjust operating profit to reflect depreciation expense, even though it is a noncash item. However, since we deduct depreciation from capital expenditures, free cash flow is truly a "cash" number. We could generate the identical free cash flow number by adding depreciation back to operating profit and deducting total capital expenditures instead of incremental investment.

7. Michael J. Mauboussin and Dan Callahan, "One Job: Expectations and the Role of Intangible Investments," *Consilient Observer: Counterpoint Global Insights*, September 15, 2020, based on Charles R. Hulten, "Decoding Microsoft: Intangible Capital as a Source of Company Growth," *NBER Working Paper 15799*, March 2010.

8. Michael Bradley and Gregg A. Jarrell, "Expected Inflation and the Constant-Growth Valuation Model," *Journal of Applied Corporate Finance* 20, no. 2 (Spring 2008): 66–78.

9. For example, liquidation value would be the best estimate of residual value for declining companies that are unlikely to endure as going concerns.

10. Here's why. Suppose shareholders invested $50 million of initial capital in a company five years ago. Over the next five years, book value grew from the initial investment of $50 million to $70 million. Market value, however, increased to $100 million over the same period. Assume that a reasonable return is 9 percent. Are shareholders satisfied with a 9 percent return on the $70 million book value, or do they expect to earn 9 percent on the $100 million market value? Investors clearly want a return on current market value.

11. Not all companies can take all their interest expense as a deduction from taxes. For companies with sales of $25 million or more, the Tax Cuts and Jobs Act of 2017 limits the interest deduction at 30 percent of earnings before interest, taxes, depreciation, and amortization (EBITDA) through 2021. Based on the figures for 2017, this would affect about 15 percent of the Russell 3000, excluding companies in the financial services and real estate sectors. From 2022 on, interest deduction will be capped at 30 percent of earnings before interest and taxes (EBIT). Based on the figures for 2017, this would affect about 20 percent of the Russell 3000, excluding companies in the financial services and real estate sectors.

12. We base our cost of equity calculations on the capital asset pricing model (CAPM). Despite repeated questions of CAPM's validity, it remains the most widely used model to quantify the relationship between risk and return. Critics offer evidence that other factors beyond beta, such as company size, market-to-book value, profitability, asset growth, and momentum, contribute to our understanding of expected long-term stock returns. Yet there is no theory to explain these results. Further, there is evidence that investors use the CAPM. (For example, see Jonathan B. Berk and Jules H. van Binsbergen, "How Do Investors Compute the Discount Rate? They Use the CAPM," *Financial Analysts' Journal* 73, no. 2 May 2017: 25–32.) We acknowledge the lively debate surrounding CAPM but do not deem its use as central to the success of the expectations investing approach.

13. By investing in a portfolio broadly representative of the overall equity market, you can diversify away substantially all the unsystematic risk, or risk that is specific to individual companies. Therefore, the market prices securities at levels that reward investors for the nondiversifiable market risk only, or the systematic risk in movements in the overall market. Beta is a measure of systematic risk.

14. These models typically assume a stream of cash flows and a forecast period and solve for the discount rate using the prevailing market price. For a detailed discussion of dividend models and expected returns, see Bradford Cornell, *The Equity Risk Premium* (New York: Wiley, 1999), chap. 3. For a

broader discussion of the cost of capital, see Shannon P. Pratt and Roger J. Grabowski, *Cost of Capital: Applications and Examples*, 5th ed. (Hoboken, NJ: Wiley, 2017).

15. Brett C. Olsen, "Firms and the Competitive Advantage Period," *Journal of Investing* 22, no. 4 (Winter 2013): 41–50.

16. Matt Krantz, "15 Companies Stockpile $1 Trillion In Cash (And Investors Want It)," *Investor's Business Daily*, March 3, 2021.

17. John R. Graham and Mark T. Leary, "The Evolution of Corporate Cash," *Review of Financial Studies* 31, no. 11 (November 2018): 4288–4344.

18. When valuing bonds or preferred stock, use market value rather than book value. Changing interest rates after issuance cause market values to diverge from book values. If, for example, interest rates rise, then market value will fall below book value. If you use book value, you will overstate the present values of bonds and preferred stocks and therefore understate shareholder value. When interest rates decline, the reverse is true. You can find current prices for publicly traded bonds and preferred stock on financial sites such as *Bloomberg*. To estimate the value of debt that does not trade publicly, discount the interest payments at the current market rate for debt of comparable risk.

19. If a pension fund is underfunded, the dollar amount of the underfunding appears on the balance sheet as a liability. If it's overfunded, it shows up as an asset.

20. We calculate the continuing value using the perpetuity-with-inflation method (see equation 2.7 in the appendix) with an expected inflation rate of 2 percent.

$$\text{Continuing value} = \frac{(\text{NOPAT})(1+\text{Inflation rate})}{(\text{Cost of capital}-\text{Inflation rate})}$$

$$= \frac{(18.12)(1.02)}{(0.08-0.02)} = \$308.04 \text{ million}$$

Discounting the above continuing value at the 8 percent cost of capital rate over the five-year period yields $209.63 million.

21. The perpetuity assumption is much less aggressive than it might appear initially, because as cash flows become more distant, their value in present value terms becomes correspondingly smaller. For example, a $1.00 perpetuity discounted at 15 percent has a value of $1.00/0.15 = $6.67. Here are the present values for annual annuities of $1.00 for periods ranging from five to twenty-five years:

Years	Present value of annuity	Percent of perpetuity value
5	$3.35	50.2%
10	5.02	75.3
15	5.85	87.7
20	6.26	93.9
25	6.46	96.9

Note that by year 10, we reach 75 percent of the perpetuity value and that by year 15, it approaches 90 percent. As the discount rate increases, the time to reach the perpetuity value decreases.

22. If we were to revise the discount rate in the perpetuity model from nominal to real terms, the valuation would equal the valuation that the perpetuity-with-inflation model generates. For example, assume a real cost of capital of 5.88 percent and expected inflation of 2 percent. The nominal cost of capital is [(1 + real cost of capital)(1 + expected inflation)] − 1. In this example, it is [(1 + 0.0588) (1 + 0.02)] − 1, or 8 percent. Now assume that free cash flow before new investment for the last year of the forecast period is $1.00. Continuing value with the perpetuity method is $1.00/0.08 = $12.50. Converting the perpetuity model from nominal to real terms, we divide the $1.00 by the real cost of capital of 5.88 percent to obtain $17.00 for continuing value, which is the same value that the perpetuity-with-inflation model generates.

3. The Expectations Infrastructure

1. Company reports and presentations. For example, see https://corporate.goodyear.com/documents/events-presentations/DB%20Global%20Auto%20Presentation%202016%20FINAL.pdf.

2. AnnaMaria Andriotis, "Another Challenge for Small Businesses: Higher Card Fees Could Be on the Way," *Wall Street Journal*, April 9, 2020.

3. Gustavo Grullon, Yelena Larkin, and Roni Michaely, "Are US Industries Becoming More Concentrated?" *Review of Finance* 23, no. 4 (July 2019): 697–743.

4. Michael E. Porter, *Competitive Advantage: Creating and Sustaining Superior Performance* (New York: The Free Press, 1985), 70–73.

5. David Besanko pointed out to us that economies of scale also might affect investments. For example, as volume grows over time, a manufacturing

company may be able to invest in larger, more automated plants that reduce its incremental investment rate. We believe that economies of scale for investment are extraordinarily difficult to assess and rarely significant in expectations investing. Consequently, we do not incorporate them in the expectations infrastructure.

6. David Besanko, David Dranove, Mark Shanley, and Scott Schaefer, *Economics of Strategy*, 7th ed. (Hoboken, NJ: Wiley, 2017), 292–295.

7. "Workday and Chiquita: Managing a Fast-Moving, Global Workforce," https://www.workday.com/content/dam/web/en-us/documents/case-studies /workday-chiquita-case-study-drove-down-costs.pdf.

8. Greg Ip, "Bringing the iPhone Assembly to the U.S. Would Be a Hollow Victory for Trump," *Wall Street Journal*, September 18, 2018.

9. For an example of how investment efficiency can lead to excess returns, see Baolian Wang, "The Cash Conversion Cycle Spread," *Journal of Financial Economics* 133, no. 2 (August 2019): 472–497.

10. In this case, we hold the required incremental investment constant.

11. The term *threshold margin* first appeared in Alfred Rappaport, "Selecting Strategies That Create Shareholder Value," *Harvard Business Review* 59, no. 3 (May–June 1981): 139–149.

12. The formula for threshold margin, using the perpetuity-with-inflation method for the continuing value, is as follows:

$$\text{Threshold margin}_t = \frac{\left(\text{Operating profit margin}_{t-1}\right)\left(1+\text{Inflation rate}\right)}{\left(1+\text{Sales growth rate}_t\right)} +$$

$$\frac{\left[\left(\text{Sales growth rate}_t\right)\right]\big/\left[\left(1+\text{Sales growth rate}_t\right)\right]\left(\begin{array}{c}\text{Incremental}\\\text{investment rate}\end{array}\right)\left(\begin{array}{c}\text{Cost}\\\text{of capital}\end{array} - \text{Inflation rate}\right)}{\left(1-\text{Cash tax rate}\right)\left(1+\text{Cost of capital}\right)}$$

where *t* equals the specified forecast year.

4. Analyzing Competitive Strategy

1. For a more comprehensive discussion of this topic, including checklists, see Michael J. Mauboussin, Dan Callahan, and Darius Majd, "Measuring the Moat: Assessing the Magnitude and Sustainability of Value Creation," *Credit Suisse Global Financial Strategies*, November 1, 2016.

2. Bruce Greenwald and Judd Kahn, *Competition Demystified: A Radically Simplified Approach to Business Strategy* (New York: Portfolio, 2005), 52–53.

3. Orit Gadiesh and James L. Gilbert, "Profit Pools: A Fresh Look at Strategy," *Harvard Business Review*, 76, no. 3 (May–June 1998): 139–147; and Orit Gadiesh and James L. Gilbert, "How to Map Your Industry's Profit Pool," *Harvard Business Review* 76, no. 3 (May–June 1998): 149–162.

4. Michael Gort, "Analysis of Stability and Change in Market Shares," *Journal of Political Economy* 71, no. 1 (February 1963): 51–63.

5. Michael E. Porter, *Competitive Strategy: Techniques for Analyzing Industries and Competitors* (New York: The Free Press, 1980), 3–33.

6. David Besanko, David Dranove, Mark Shanley, and Scott Schaefer, *Economics of Strategy*, 7th ed. (Hoboken, NJ: Wiley, 2017), 186–211.

7. Sharon M. Oster, *Modern Competitive Analysis* (Oxford: Oxford University Press, 1999), 57–82.

8. Besanko et al., *Economics of Strategy*, 111–112.

9. Clayton M. Christensen, *The Innovator's Dilemma: When New Technologies Cause Great Firms to Fail* (Boston: Harvard Business School Press, 1997).

10. Christensen, *The Innovator's Dilemma*, 32.

11. Andrew S. Grove, *Only the Paranoid Survive* (New York: Currency/Doubleday, 1996).

12. Larry Downes and Paul Nunes, "Blockbuster Becomes a Casualty of Big Bang Disruption," *Harvard Business Review Online*, November 7, 2013, https://hbr.org/2013/11/blockbuster-becomes-a-casualty-of-big-bang-disruption.

13. Frank Olito, "The Rise and Fall of Blockbuster," *Business Insider*, August 20, 2020, https://www.businessinsider.com/rise-and-fall-of-blockbuster.

14. Adam M. Brandenburger and Harborne W. Stuart Jr., "Value-Based Business Strategy," *Journal of Economics and Management Strategy* 5, no.1 (Spring 1996): 5–24.

15. Michael E. Porter, *Competitive Advantage: Creating and Sustaining Superior Performance* (New York: The Free Press, 1985), 36.

16. Joan Magretta, *Understanding Michael Porter: The Essential Guide to Competition and Strategy* (Boston: Harvard Business Review Press, 2012), 73.

17. Carl Shapiro and Hal R. Varian, *Information Rules: A Strategic Guide to the Network Economy* (Boston: Harvard Business School Press, 1999).

18. W. Brian Arthur, "Increasing Returns and the New World of Business," *Harvard Business Review* 74, no. 4 (July–August 1996): 101–109.

19. Shapiro and Varian, *Information Rules*, 117.

20. Daniel M. McCarthy, Peter S. Fader, and Bruce G. S. Hardie, "Valuing Subscription-Based Businesses Using Publicly Disclosed Customer Data," *Journal of Marketing* 81, no. 1 (January 2017): 17–35.

21. Daniel M. McCarthy and Peter S. Fader, "How to Value a Company by Analyzing Its Customers," *Harvard Business Review* 98, no. 1 (January–February 2020): 51–55.

5. How to Estimate Price-Implied Expectations

1. Warren E. Buffett, "How Inflation Swindles the Equity Investor," *Fortune*, May 1977, 250–267.

2. Aswath Damodaran's website offers a full cost of capital discussion and many complementary tools. See http://www.stern.nyu.edu/~adamodar.

3. See Merton H. Miller and Franco Modigliani, "Dividend Policy, Growth, and the Valuation of Shares," *Journal of Business* 34, no. 4 (October 1961): 411–433. The market-implied forecast period was introduced under the name *value growth duration* in Alfred Rappaport, *Creating Shareholder Value: The New Standard for Business Performance* (New York: The Free Press, 1986). For a detailed discussion of the role of the market-implied forecast period in security analysis, see Michael Mauboussin and Paul Johnson, "Competitive Advantage Period: The Neglected Value Driver," *Financial Management* 26, no. 2 (Summer 1997): 67–74. The authors call the forecast period the *competitive advantage period*. For a discussion of fade rate, see David A. Holland and Bryant A. Matthews, *Beyond Earnings: Applying the HOLT CFROI and Economic Profit Framework* (Hoboken, NJ: Wiley, 2017).

4. Brett C. Olsen, "Firms and the Competitive Advantage Period," *Journal of Investing* 22, no. 4 (Winter 2013): 41–50.

5. Plantronics, Inc., Form 8-K, November 4, 2019.

6. Identifying Expectations Opportunities

1. Don A. Moore, *Perfectly Confident: How to Calibrate Your Decisions Wisely* (New York: Harper Business, 2020).

2. J. Edward Russo and Paul J. H. Schoemaker, "Managing Overconfidence," *Sloan Management Review* 33, no. 2 (Winter 1992): 7–17.

3. Raymond S. Nickerson, "Confirmation Bias: A Ubiquitous Phenomenon in Many Guises," *Review of General Psychology* 2, no. 2 (June 1998): 175–220; and Chu Xin Cheng, "Confirmation Bias in Investments," *International Journal of Economics and Finance* 11, no. 2 (February 2019): 50–55.

4. Domino's Pizza, Inc., 10-K, 2019.

5. Steve Gerhardt, Sue Joiner, and Ed Dittfurth, "An Analysis of Expected Potential Returns from Selected Pizza Franchises," *Journal of Business and Educational Leadership* 8, no. 1 (Fall 2018): 101–111.

7. Buy, Sell, or Hold?

1. Going from expected values for a series of investments to constructing a portfolio is more complex than simply picking the securities with the highest expected values. But the inputs into the calculation of expected value are useful in portfolio construction. See chapter 6 in Harry M. Markowitz, *Portfolio Selection: Efficient Diversification of Investments* (New York: Wiley, 1959).

2. Daniel Kahneman, *Thinking, Fast and Slow* (New York: Farrar, Straus and Giroux, 2011), 245–254.

3. Michael J. Mauboussin, Dan Callahan, and Darius Majd, "The Base Rate Book: Integrating the Past to Better Anticipate the Future," *Credit Suisse: Global Financial Strategies*, September 26, 2016.

4. We use the term *excess return* to depict returns for an individual stock that are higher than the cost of capital. We use the term *superior returns* throughout the book as performance above an appropriate benchmark for an investor's entire stock portfolio.

5. Assume a $100 expected value, a current stock price of $80 (80 percent of expected value), and a 6 percent cost of equity capital. We obtain the expected value two years from now, $112.36, by taking today's $100 expected value and compounding it at the 6 percent cost of equity capital rate. If the $80 stock price rises to $112.36 at the end of the two years, the annual return is 18.5 percent. Subtracting the cost of equity gives an excess return of 12.5 percentage points.

6. Richard H. Thaler, "Anomalies: Saving, Fungibility, and Mental Accounts," *Journal of Economic Perspectives* 4, no. 1 (Winter 1990): 193–205.

7. Hersh Shefrin, *Beyond Greed and Fear: Understanding Behavioral Finance and the Psychology of Investing* (Boston: Harvard Business School Press, 2000), 214–218.

8. Klakow Akepanidtaworn, Rick Di Mascio, Alex Imas, and Lawrence Schmidt, "Selling Fast and Buying Slow: Heuristics and Trading Performance of Institutional Investors," *Working Paper*, February 2021, available at SSRN, https://dx.doi.org/10.2139/ssrn.3301277.

9. Daniel Kahneman and Amos Tversky, "Prospect Theory: An Analysis of Decision Under Risk," *Econometrica* 47, no. 2 (March 1979): 263–291.

10. John W. Payne, Suzanne B. Shu, Elizabeth C. Webb, and Namika Sagara, "Development of an Individual Measure of Loss Aversion," *Association for Consumer Research Proceedings* 43 (October 2015); and Christoph Merkle, "Financial Loss Aversion Illusion," *Review of Finance* 24, no. 2 (March 2020): 381–413.

11. Baba Shiv, George Loewenstein, Antoine Bechara, Hanna Damasio, and Antonio R. Damasio, "Investment Behavior and the Negative Side of Emotion," *Psychological Science* 16, no. 6 (June 2005): 435–439.

12. This analysis applies to taxable investment accounts and not to tax-deferred accounts such as 401(k)s.

13. As we write this, 20 percent is the long-term U.S. federal capital gains tax rate for those in the highest tax bracket. Other federal and state taxes may apply, which make the consideration of taxes even more relevant.

8. Beyond Discounted Cash Flow

1. We are indebted to Martha Amram for helping us develop these techniques.

2. For readers who want to learn more about how to identify and value real options, see Martha Amram and Nalin Kulatilaka, *Real Options: Managing Strategic Investment in an Uncertain World* (Boston: Harvard Business School Press, 1999); and Jonathan Mun, *Real Options Analysis: Tools and Techniques for Valuing Strategic Investments and Decisions with Integrated Risk Management and Advanced Quantitative Decision Analytics*, 3rd ed. (Dublin, CA: Thomson-Shore and ROV Press, 2016).

3. Nalin Kulatilaka and Alan J. Marcus, "Project Valuation Under Uncertainty: When Does DCF Fail?," *Journal of Applied Corporate Finance* 5, no. 3 (Fall 1992): 92–100; and Alexander B. van Putten and Ian MacMillan, "Making Real Options Really Work," *Harvard Business Review* 82, no. 12 (December 2004): 134–141.

4. The option to abandon is analogous to a put option.

5. Dividend payments also affect option value. We set aside dividends to simplify this example.

6. Richard A. Brealey and Stewart C. Myers, *Principles of Corporate Finance*, 5th ed. (New York: Irwin McGraw Hill, 1996), appendix 12–13.

7. A European call option assumes that the exercise decision occurs only at option expiration. American options assume that the exercise decision can come at any time during the option's life. The European and American call values are identical in this case given that there are no dividend payments.

8. Net present value = $S - X = 0$ means that $S = X$. Accordingly, $S/X = 1$.

9. Steven R. Grenadier, "Option Exercise Games: The Intersection of Real Options and Game Theory," *Journal of Applied Corporate Finance* 13, no. 2 (Summer 2000): 99–107.

10. It is important to consider these past investments, especially when a company is investing in mergers and acquisitions or joint ventures. Acquisitions of small companies by large companies often do not appear to add value, but may have substantial real option value in the form of economies of scope. See Xiaohui Gao, Jay R. Ritter, and Zhongyan Zhu, "Where Have All the IPOs Gone?" *Journal of Financial and Quantitative Analysis* 48, no. 6 (December 2013): 1663–1692.

11. Look at the price of the option and the other four inputs. Use the valuation formula to solve for the level of volatility consistent with the trading price of the option. See Amram and Kulatilaka, *Real Options*, for how to estimate volatility. See www.ivolatilty.com for current volatility estimates using these two methods.

12. This is the case for companies that enter into businesses that are markedly different from their core operations.

13. These figures are from September 2020.

14. Since the magnitude of expected value creation for the established businesses is insufficient to account for the stock price, the model must compensate by artificially extending the duration of value creation.

15. Josh Tarasoff and John McCormack, "How to Create Value Without Earnings: The Case of Amazon," *Journal of Applied Corporate Finance* 25, no. 3 (Summer 2013): 39–43.

16. Company managers can help this process by telling a great story. See Aswath Damodaran, *Narrative and Numbers: The Value of Stories in Business* (New York: Columbia Business School, 2017).

17. George Soros, *The Alchemy of Finance: Reading the Mind of the Market* (New York: Wiley, 1994), 49.

18. In a secondary offering, public investors supply financing as a company sells new shares. In an acquisition financed with stock, the buyer issues new shares to finance the deal.

19. Sanjeev Bhojraj, "Stock Compensation Expense, Cash Flows, and Inflated Valuations," *Review of Accounting Studies* 25, no. 3 (September 2020): 1078–1097.

9. Across the Economic Landscape

1. Feng Gu and Baruch Lev, *The End of Accounting and the Path Forward for Investors and Managers* (Hoboken, NJ: Wiley, 2016).

2. Sara Castellanos, "Nasdaq Ramps Up Cloud Move," *Wall Street Journal*, September 15, 2020.

3. Paul M. Romer, "Endogenous Technological Change," *Journal of Political Economy* 98, no. 5 (1990): S71–S102.

4. Kai-Fu Lee, *AI Superpowers: China, Silicon Valley, and the New World Order* (Boston: Houghton Mifflin Harcourt, 2018), 22–26.

5. Carl Shapiro and Hal R. Varian, *Information Rules: A Strategic Guide to the Network Economy* (Boston: Harvard Business School Press, 1999), 179.

6. The tipping point is a related idea. The term refers to the level of market share at which future market share gains become cheaper to acquire, leading a single firm or technology to overcome all others. For a given product, the tipping point is equivalent to reaching critical mass, a level of market share that ensures success. A market is likely to tip if there is low demand for variety and high economies of scale. Low demand for variety means that the market accepts either a formal or a de facto standard. In contrast, standardization in other knowledge industries, such as drugs, doesn't make much sense. Consumers need a variety of solutions for their health care needs.

7. Investors must first identify sectors where network effects are intense. Strong network effects tend to occur when the network participants enjoy a high degree of interactivity and compatibility. Next, investors must find the companies most likely to translate the benefits of network effects into shareholder value.

8. For a detailed discussion, see Geoffrey A. Moore, *Crossing the Chasm: Marketing and Selling High-Tech Products to Mainstream Customers* (New York: HarperBusiness, 1991).

9. Goksin Kavlak, James McNerney, and Jessika Trancik, "Evaluating the Causes of Cost Reduction in Photovoltaic Modules," *Energy Policy* 123 (December 2018): 700–710.

10. Joseph A. DiMasi, Henry G. Grabowski, and Ronald W. Hansen, "Innovation in the Pharmaceutical Industry: New Estimates of R&D Costs," *Journal of Health Economics* 47 (May 2016): 20–33.

11. Transcript from O'Reilly Automotive Inc. at Goldman Sachs Retail Conference, September 10, 2020, https://corporate.oreillyauto.com/cmsstatic/ORLY_Transcript_2020-09-10.pdf.

12. David Besanko, David Dranove, Mark Shanley, and Scott Schaefer, *Economics of Strategy*, 7th ed. (Hoboken, NJ: Wiley, 2017), 70–73. This concept is also known as Wright's law. See Béla Nagy, J. Doyne Farmer, Quan M. Bui, and Jessika E. Trancik, "Statistical Basis for Predicting Technological Progress," *PLoS ONE* 8, no. 2 (2013).

13. Besanko et al., *Economics of Strategy*, 66–67. Also, see Morton A. Meyers, *Happy Accidents: Serendipity in Modern Medical Breakthroughs* (New York: Arcade, 2007).

14. Kimberly-Clark Investor Presentation. Financial information as of December 31, 2019.

15. Reed Hastings and Erin Meyer, *No Rules Rules: Netflix and the Culture of Reinvention* (New York: Penguin Press, 2020), 4–8; and Netflix financial statements.

16. Ashlee Vance, "A.M.D. to Split into Two Operations," *New York Times*, October 6, 2008.

17. Recall that service and knowledge businesses expense most of their investments, and therefore efficiencies related to these investments are considered to be cost efficiencies.

18. Marshall Fisher, Vishal Gaur, and Herb Kleinberger, "Curing the Addiction to Growth," *Harvard Business Review* 95, no. 1 (January–February 2017): 66–74.

10. Mergers and Acquisitions

1. Bob Haas and Angus Hodgson, "M&A Deal Evaluation: Challenging Metrics Myths," *Institute for Mergers, Acquisitions and Alliances*, A. T. Kearney, 2013.

2. Sometimes an acquisition represents part of a more global long-term strategy to attain a competitive advantage. What is important is that the overall strategy adds a satisfactory level of value. In such a situation, the acquiring company may not expect a particular purchase to contribute value but purchasing may be the only feasible way to execute the strategy. Such an acquisition does not represent an end in itself; rather, it provides the real option to participate in future value-generating opportunities. Expectations investors should, however, be wary of CEOs who use real options rhetoric to rationalize poorly conceived acquisitions or overpayments. For a comprehensive treatment of the difficulty of producing synergies, see Mark L. Sirower, *The Synergy Trap* (New York: The Free Press, 1997).

3. When the seller is publicly traded, market value is the best basis for establishing stand-alone value. Market value may not be a particularly good proxy for stand-alone value for companies whose stocks have been bid up in anticipation of a takeover. To estimate stand-alone value, deduct the "takeover premium" impounded in the current market price from the current market price.

4. For more on the Dow Chemical deal, see Michael J. Mauboussin, *Think Twice: Harnessing the Power of Counterintuition* (Boston: Harvard Business Press, 2009), 7–8.

5. Scott A. Christofferson, Robert S. McNish, and Diane L. Sias, "Where Mergers Go Wrong," *McKinsey Quarterly* (May 2004): 1–6.

6. This section is adapted from Alfred Rappaport and Mark L. Sirower, "Stock or Cash? The Trade-Offs for Buyers and Sellers in Mergers and Acquisitions," *Harvard Business Review* 77, no. 6 (November–December 1999): 147–158.

7. Rappaport and Sirower, "Stock or Cash?," 156–158.

8. Peter J. Clark and Roger W. Mills, *Masterminding the Deal: Breakthroughs in M&A Strategy and Analysis* (London: Kogan Page, 2013).

9. Tim Loughran and Anand M. Vijh, "Do Long-Term Shareholders Benefit from Corporate Acquisitions?," *Journal of Finance* 52, no. 5 (December 1997): 1765–1790.

10. Pavel G. Savor and Qi Lu, "Do Stock Mergers Create Value for Acquirers?," *Journal of Finance* 64, no. 3 (June 2009): 1061–1097.

11. Merger arbitrageurs are willing to assume this risk in return for the opportunity to earn the spread between the stock price and the offer. As a result, this discount is known as an arbitrage spread.

12. While the market's short-term response to a merger announcement provides a reasonably reliable barometer of the likely consequences of the transaction, with hindsight the market assessment just might turn out to be incorrect. Research has shown that the market's assessments are unbiased. This means that, on average, the market neither overvalues nor undervalues the transaction. We can view the collective judgment of investors as an objective assessment of the merger's value to buying and selling shareholders. In other words, the immediate price reaction is the market's best estimate of the long-term implications of the transaction. See Mark L. Sirower and Sumit Sahni, "Avoiding the 'Synergy Trap': Practical Guidance on M&A Decisions for CEOs and Boards," *Journal of Applied Corporate Finance* 18, no. 3 (Summer 2006): 83–95.

11. Share Buybacks

1. Companies finance these programs through internally generated cash flow, cash on the balance sheet, or issuance of debt.

2. Alberto Manconi, Urs Peyer, and Theo Vermaelen, "Are Buybacks Good for Long-Term Shareholder Value? Evidence from Buybacks Around

the World," *Journal of Financial and Quantitative Analysis* 54, no. 5 (October 2019): 1899–1935.

3. William Lazonick, "Profits Without Prosperity," *Harvard Business Review* 92, no. 9 (September 2014): 46–55. For a proper response, see Jesse M. Fried and Charles C. Y. Wang, "Are Buybacks Really Shortchanging Investment?," *Harvard Business Review* 96, no. 2 (March–April 2018): 88–95.

4. As Warren Buffett wrote in Berkshire Hathaway's 1984 annual report, "When companies with outstanding businesses and comfortable financial positions find their shares selling far below intrinsic value in the marketplace, no alternative action can benefit shareholders as surely as repurchases." See Berkshire Hathaway Inc., Letter to shareholders, 1984, https://www .berkshirehathaway.com/letters/1984.html.

5. Zicheng Lei and Chendi Zhang, "Leveraged Buybacks," *Journal of Corporate Finance* 39 (August 2016): 242–262.

6. Michael C. Jensen, "Corporate Control and the Politics of Finance," *Journal of Applied Corporate Finance* 4, no. 2 (Summer 1991): 13–34.

7. Walter I. Boudry, Jarl G. Kallberg, and Crocker H. Liu, "Investment Opportunities and Share Repurchases," *Journal of Corporate Finance* 23 (December 2013): 23–38; and Mark Mietzner, "Why Do Firms Decide to Stop Their Share Repurchase Programs?," *Review of Managerial Science* 11, no. 4 (October 2017): 815–855.

8. Ahmet C. Kurt, "Managing EPS and Signaling Undervaluation as a Motivation for Repurchases: The Case of Accelerated Share Repurchases," *Review of Accounting and Finance* 17, no. 4 (November 2018): 453–481.

9. Companies and investors often incorrectly associate the "return" from a buyback with accounting-based measures, such as the inverse of the P/E multiple. The (faulty) logic is as follows: Say the consensus expects a company to earn $1 per share. The shares trade at $25, a P/E ratio of 25. So the company gets $1 in earnings for every $25 share it buys back for a "return" of 4 percent (1/25). The flaw is that investors cannot reliably link a P/E multiple to the cost of equity because multiples are a shorthand that incorporate variables other than the discount rate. These variables include sales growth, operating margins, investment needs, and the sustainability of competitive advantage.

10. Alfred Rappaport, *Creating Shareholder Value: The New Standard for Business Performance* (New York: The Free Press, 1986), 96.

11. Reinvestment opportunities range from relatively high returns to returns modestly above the cost of capital. Naturally, management should target lower return opportunities for further scrutiny. However, some investments with a low rate of return, such as those for environmental controls, may be regulated and therefore unavoidable. Other investments appear to

generate relatively low returns until you consider the consequences of not investing. Yet other investments may not fully incorporate the benefits to other products or services in the calculations of the rate of return.

12. Alon Brav, John R. Graham, Campbell R. Harvey, and Roni Michaely, "Payout Policy in the 21st Century," *Journal of Financial Economics* 77, no. 3 (September 2015): 483–527.

13. Manconi, Peyer, and Vermaelen, "Are Buybacks Good for Long-Term Shareholder Value?"

14. In 1982, the Securities and Exchange Commission enacted Rule 10b-18, which provided a safe harbor for open-market share repurchases provided companies followed specified rules. Prior to 1982, companies that repurchased shares ran the risk of being charged with stock manipulation. The safe harbor rules have been updated over time to accommodate changes in the market.

15. See "Frequently Asked Questions Provided by Microsoft Corporation to Employees" at https://www.sec.gov/Archives/edgar/data/789019 /000119312506150261/dex995.htm.

16. Ranjan D'Emello and Pervin K. Shroff, "Equity Undervaluation and Decisions Related to Repurchase Tender Offers: An Empirical Investigation," *Journal of Finance* 55, no. 5 (October 2000): 2399–2424.

17. Theo Vermaelen, "Common Stock Repurchases and Market Signaling," *Journal of Financial Economics* 9, no. 2 (June 1981): 139–183.

18. Jacob Oded and Allen Michel, "Stock Repurchases and the EPS Enhancement Fallacy," *Financial Analysts' Journal* 64, no. 4 (July–August 2008): 62–75.

19. John R. Graham, Campbell R. Harvey, and Shiva Rajgopal, "Value Destruction and Financial Reporting Decisions," *Financial Analysts' Journal* 62, no. 6 (November–December 2006): 27–39.

20. Bruce Dravis, "Dilution, Disclosure, Equity Compensation, and Buybacks," *Business Lawyer* 74, no. 3 (Summer 2019): 631–658.

21. Michael Rapoport and Theo Francis, "Share Buybacks Help Lift Corporate Earnings," *Wall Street Journal*, September 23, 2018.

22. The results are the same if we assume instead that the companies borrow to fund the program.

23. Roni Michaely and Amani Moin, "Disappearing and Reappearing Dividends," SSRN Working Paper, July 2020, https://dx.doi.org/10.2139/ssrn .3067550.

24. Our statements relate to the United States. Other countries have different tax rates and policies.

25. For a more sophisticated approach, see John R. Graham, "How Big Are the Tax Benefits of Debt?," *Journal of Finance* 55, no. 5 (October 2000):

1901–1941. As we pointed out in note 11 from chapter 2, not all companies can take all their interest expense as a deduction from taxes. For companies with sales of $25 million or more, the Tax Cuts and Jobs Act of 2017 limits the interest deduction at 30 percent of earnings before interest, taxes, depreciation, and amortization (EBITDA) through 2021. Based on the figures for 2017, this would affect about 15 percent of the Russell 3000, excluding companies in the financial services and real estate sectors. From 2022 on, interest deduction will be capped at 30 percent of earnings before interest and taxes (EBIT). Based on the figures for 2017, this would affect about 20 percent of the Russell 3000, excluding companies in the financial services and real estate sectors.

12. Sources of Expectations Opportunities

1. Gary Klein, "Performing a Project Premortem," *Harvard Business Review* 85, no. 9 (September 2007): 18–19.

2. Andrew Mauboussin and Michael J. Mauboussin, "If You Say Something Is 'Likely,' How Likely Do People Think It Is?," *Harvard Business Review Online*, July 3, 2018.

3. Allan H. Murphy and Harald Daan, "Impacts of Feedback and Experience on the Quality of Subjective Probability Forecasts: Comparison of Results from the First and Second Years of the Zierikzee Experiment," *Monthly Weather Review* 112, no. 3 (March 1984): 413–423.

4. Philip E. Tetlock, *Expert Political Judgment: How Good Is It? How Can We Know?* (Princeton, NJ: Princeton University Press, 2005).

5. Stefano Ramelli and Alexander F. Wagner, "Feverish Stock Price Reactions to COVID-19," *Review of Corporate Finance Studies* 9, no. 3 (November 2020): 622–655.

6. Jerold B. Warner, Ross L. Watts, and Karen H. Wruck, "Stock Prices and Top Management Changes," *Journal of Financial Economics* 20 (January–March 1988): 461–492.

7. William Thorndike, *The Outsiders: Eight Unconventional CEOs and Their Radically Rational Blueprint for Success* (Boston: Harvard Business Review Press, 2012).

8. Scott Davis, Carter Copeland, and Rob Wertheimer, *Lessons from the Titans: What Companies in the New Economy Can Learn from the Industrial Giants to Drive Sustainable Success* (New York: McGraw Hill, 2020), 119–151.

9. Davis, Copeland, and Wertheimer, *Lessons from the Titans*, 1–48.

10. Boris Groysberg, *Chasing Stars: The Myth of Talent and the Portability of Performance* (Princeton, NJ: Princeton University Press, 2010), 324–326.

11. Gary Smith, "Stock Splits: A Reevaluation," *Journal of Investing* 28, no. 4 (June 2019): 21–29.

12. Fengyu Li, Mark H. Liu, and Yongdong (Eric) Shia, "Institutional Ownership Around Stock Splits," *Pacific-Basin Finance Journal* 46 (December 2017): 14–40.

13. Alon Brav, John R. Graham, Campbell R. Harvey, and Roni Michaely, "Payout Policy in the 21st Century," *Journal of Financial Economics* 77, no. 3 (September 2005): 483–527.

14. Doron Nissim and Amir Ziv, "Dividend Changes and Future Profitability," *Journal of Finance* 56, no. 6 (December 2001): 2111–2133.

15. Roni Michaely, Stefano Rossi, and Michael Weber, *Signaling Safety*, ECGI Finance Working Paper No. 653/2020, February 2020, https://dx.doi.org/10.2139/ssrn.3064029.

16. Kent Daniel and Sheridan Titman, "Another Look at Market Responses to Tangible and Intangible Information," *Critical Finance Review* 5, no. 1 (May 2016): 165–175.

17. Michael J. Cooper, Huseyin Gulen, and Michael J. Schill, "Asset Growth and the Cross-Section of Stock Returns," *Journal of Finance* 63, no. 4 (August 2008): 1609–1651. For non-U.S. results, see Akiko Watanabe, Yan Xu, Tong Yao, and Tong Yu, "The Asset Growth Effect: Insights for International Equity Markets," *Journal of Financial Economics* 108, no. 2 (May 2013): 259–263.

18. Matteo Arena and Stephen Ferris, "A Survey of Litigation in Corporate Finance," *Managerial Finance* 43, no.1 (2017): 4–18; and Amar Gande and Craig M. Lewis, "Shareholder-Initiated Class Action Lawsuits: Shareholder Wealth Effects and Industry Spillovers," *Journal of Financial and Quantitative Analysis* 44, no. 4 (August 2009): 823–850.

19. Joe Nocera, "BP Is Still Paying for the Deepwater Horizon Spill," *Bloomberg*, February 4, 2020, https://www.bloomberg.com/news/articles/2020-02-04/bp-is-still-paying-for-the-deepwater-horizon-spill.

20. George Washington Regulatory Studies Center, "Reg Stats," https://regulatorystudies.columbian.gwu.edu/reg-stats.

21. Michail Batikas, Stefan Bechtold, Tobias Kretschmer, and Christian Peukert, *European Privacy Law and Global Markets for Data*, CEPR Discussion Paper No. DP14475, March 25, 2020, https://ssrn.com/abstract=3560282.

22. James M. McTaggart, Peter W. Kontes, and Michael C. Mankins, *The Value Imperative: Managing for Superior Shareholder Returns* (New York: The Free Press, 1994), 241.

23. Donghum "Don" Lee and Ravi Madhavan, "Divestiture and Firm Performance: A Meta-Analysis," *Journal of Management* 36, no. 6 (November 2010): 1345–1371.

24. Michael J. Mauboussin, Dan Callahan, David Rones, and Sean Burns, "Managing the Man Overboard Moment: Making an Informed Decision After a Large Price Drop," *Credit Suisse: Global Financial Strategies*, January 15, 2015.

25. Momentum combines prior stock-price moves and earnings revisions. Valuation reflects the gap between price and value in a cash flow model. And quality assesses whether a company has made investments that earn a return above the cost of capital. For more details, see Mauboussin, Callahan, Rones, and Burns, "Managing the Man Overboard Moment," 18–19.

26. Michael J. Mauboussin, Dan Callahan, Darius Majd, Greg Williamson, and David Rones, "Celebrating the Summit: Making an Informed Decision After a Large Price Gain," *Credit Suisse: Global Financial Strategies*, January 11, 2016.

Index

Page numbers in *italics* indicate figures or tables.

241